# *Bling, Blogs and Bluetooth*

## Modern Living for Oldies

Edited by Nick Parker

**With an introduction by Richard Ingrams**

PROFILE BOOKS

First published in Great Britain in 2006 by
Profile Books Ltd
3a Exmouth House
Pine Street
Exmouth Market
London EC1R 0JH
*www.profilebooks.co.uk*



A CIP catalogue record for this book is available from the British Library.

ISBN-10: 1 86197 824 3
ISBN-13: 978 1 86197 824 0

Text design by Sue Lamble

Printed and bound in Great Britain by Bookmarque Ltd, Croydon, Surrey

# Contents

# Acknowledgements

*The Oldie* would like to thank all the authors who kindly agreed to their work being reproduced in this book. We also gratefully acknowledge the following cartoonists who have given permission for their artwork to be reprinted: Ray Chesterton, Cluff, Will Dawbarn, Nick Hobart, Holland, Ray Jelliffe, Kathryn Lamb, Mason, McNeil, Mico, Mike Oaker, PAK, Pat, Royston, Russell, Spittle and Colin Wheeler. Finally, many thanks to all *Oldie* readers who submitted examples of irritating modern phrases. That's all, innit.

# Introduction

Richard Ingrams

WHEN I STARTED *THE OLDIE* IN 1992 the aim was to provide readers with some sort of antidote to the cult of youth which still dominates our media – and everything else for that matter.

There was another raison d'être for the new magazine. Like many of my generation (b. 1937), I was very much aware that a strange new world had come into being, leaving oldies baffled and resentful. Many of the things with which we were brought up were fast disappearing. Massive supermarkets had replaced little shops. Cinemas had fifteen different films showing, in place of the traditional one. Bus conductors had vanished. Journalists had left Fleet Street and were now working from skyscrapers in Canary Wharf. Men and women no longer got married, they had 'partners'.

The other thing that made matters worse was the sheer speed of technological change – no sooner had we thrown away our LPs and got used to cassettes, than they too were declared redundant. CDs had arrived and we were told that they were scratch proof and virtually indestructible. It wasn't true. Never mind, because after only a brief interlude the iPod is with us, capable apparently of storing in its tiny confines all the music you could ever wish to listen to. How long before that too is declared obsolete?

Then there were videos which were supposed to enable you to record your favourite programmes when you were asleep or out to drinks with the neighbours. The technology proved beyond the grasp of oldie folk and only small children seemed to be able to master it. But within a year or two videos themselves were out, to be replaced by DVDs. Indistinguishable from CDs, they required their own special machine complete with special remote. This could then be added to the other remotes required to operate the TV set, with a guarantee that the one you wanted would be hidden beneath a cushion on the settee.

Technological advancement was supposed to make life simpler. In fact it was making it more complicated – in certain areas at any rate. It was also giving rise to aggravation on many fronts. A train journey was no longer the soothing experience it once had been, thanks to the loud-mouthed bores talking on their mobile phones. If you managed to nod off the chances were that you would be woken by a shrill ring or the opening of Mozart's G minor symphony (arranged for computer).

Modern technology was meanwhile taking a lot of the fun out of life. People said how wonderful it was to be able to track down out-of-print books instantly via the Internet. But didn't that take away the excitement of searching for them in bookshops the length and breadth of Britain?

Even when the system seemed to have improved, there was a snag. You could now get your cash out of a hole in the wall at any hour of the day or night, but if you wanted to have a word with the bank manager – once a readily accessible figure – you would most likely find yourself talking to a strange woman in India. You might even be told that your call was being monitored 'for training purposes'.

Perhaps you should have felt lucky merely to be in contact with a live human being, because elsewhere the machine, or the computer, was taking over. All information was obtainable on the Internet on something called Google. There was no longer any call for libraries. Metallic, pre-recorded voices at railway stations apologised for trains being late or warned you to be on the lookout for suspicious packages. Behind it all lay the mysterious science of 'customer care', which aimed to lull the 'customer' – which is what railway passengers and hospital patients were now called – into thinking that their welfare was a matter of paramount importance to the computers running the system.

It was all increasingly baffling. In every field, mysterious new words and phrases had come into being. In politics, for example, we now had spin doctors and focus groups, not to mention soundbites. What did it all mean? The business world was even stranger. The suited men who could be overheard on trains talking loudly on their mobiles spoke of the need to be 'proactive'; they had a desire to 'touch base'. Peculiar new customs such as 'dress-down Friday' had been introduced. Letters from the bank or the solicitors might carry a strange wreath-like device with the legend, 'Investors in People'.

The bulk of these phenomena had no doubt originated in the USA, home of most daft concepts. But, surprisingly, a great many novelties had an Oriental origin. Children had discarded their traditional teddy bears and dolls and carried about with them strange robotic keyrings known as tamagotchi – a baby substitute that required constant attention (food and nappy changing) in order to stay alive. The grown-ups meanwhile were re-arranging their furniture in accordance with a mysterious Chinese system called Feng Shui, or trying to keep calm with something called Reiki therapy.

In the first years of the new century a new craze overtook not only this country but, it seemed, the entire world: Sudoku fooled people into thinking that it too was the invention of a Japanese mastermind whereas, in fact, as an article in this book explains, it originated in Switzerland. Whatever its origin, it soon proved dangerously addictive. Men and women of all ages could be seen crouched over the Sudoku squares, graded according to their difficulty into 'elementary', 'intermediate' or even 'fiendish'.

Were we becoming more rational and progressive, as the optimists maintained? On the contrary – among all the innovations and the technical wizardry, a strong element of lunacy could be discerned. There were any number of new cults and religions, while millions appeared to take seriously the claims of *The Da Vinci Code*, which proposed the unlikely theory that Jesus had been married to Mary Magdalene, that they had had children and that the story had been suppressed for centuries by a host of powerful VIPs including Leonardo da Vinci and Sir Isaac Newton. Despite proof that the story had originated in a hoax, the book sold millions and inspired a host of spin-offs and even a whole new branch of literature known as 'Alternative History' (i.e: fiction).

Perhaps the passion for Alternative History had something to do with the fact that people had lost their interest in the real thing. 'The past is a foreign country. They do things differently there,' L. P. Hartley famously said at the beginning of *The Go-Between*. But it is a country that young people show no particular wish to travel to. All that matters is Now, and the possibility that the way things are now might be related to the things that happened long ago, or even quite recently, is not considered. 'That was before my time' is sufficient reason for not knowing about it.

Oldies, of course, have links with the past, and as such are likely to be overlooked. But that is no good reason why they should retreat into their shells: they need to find out about the world, if only to know their enemy.

They need to have the necessary information to be in a position to disillusion the young and cultivate a healthy attitude of cynicism.

We at *The Oldie* have tried, with the help of our own team of expert writers, to provide the older generation with some of the necessary ammunition to engage with the young. As somebody said, knowledge is power.

## Affluenza

Life in the ghetto is tough. Its gutters are awash with booze and drugs. Depression and suicide are not uncommon. Its inhabitants frequently live shattered, helpless lives, shunned and despised by the rest of society. But this is not an inner-city ghetto, and its inhabitants are not the poverty-stricken or the homeless. These sorry specimens are the rich. This is life within the 'golden ghetto'.

The term was coined by an American, Jessie H. O'Neill, in her 1997 book of the same name. It is a self-help book for the rich, to help them cope with the potential traumas of being wealthy, which, it turns out, extend far beyond deciding which hat to wear at Ascot, or choosing to which gold card to charge the new Bentley.

New studies are showing the potential psychological damage that wealth – especially inherited wealth – can cause if it is not handled responsibly. O'Neill sees these problems in terms of a sickness, which she calls 'affluenza'. The symptoms range from the general feelings of directionlessness one can get from not needing to work in order to survive to the more serious problems some rich people have in forming healthy personal relationships, often stemming from the fact that most of their childhood was spent being tended to by servants, with little parental closeness. The instant gratification that becomes the norm when you have the money to fulfil your every whim often leads to an inability to cope with everyday frustrations or setbacks. (That's why the rich are bad at queuing.)

Perhaps most damaging of all is the ease with which money allows people to retreat from their problems, often into drink or drug addiction. And the limitless supplies of money mean that the natural 'rock bottom' that can force addicts on to the road to recovery is often never reached. This is life in the golden ghetto, trapped and controlled by your own fortune.

Well my heart bleeds, it really does. Having spent two years working in a bookshop in achingly wealthy South Kensington (Customer: 'You don't understand – I must have two copies of everything; one for the town, and one for the country'), it has to be said that on hearing the news that those arrogant, obnoxious folk (who were indeed bad at queuing) might be having a rough time of it, sympathy did not feature highly on my list of emotional responses. I believe that punching the air and whooping ungenerously about sweet revenge may have snuck in ahead of concerned empathy.

Disarmingly, O'Neill anticipates my response as a perfectly natural one, and sees it as part of the problem: the symptoms of affluenza are often not taken seriously, or else seen as 'the price that has to be paid' for wealth. This also signifies a paradox in many people's attitude to money. While we are not surprised when the tabloids reveal that another lottery winner's life has fallen apart due to the sudden burden of several million pounds, many of us still hanker after riches.

It is at this point that O'Neill broadens her definition of affluenza sufferers to include any individual whose life is controlled by the desire for great wealth. Symptoms include workaholism; an equation of increased material wealth with increased happiness; one's self-esteem being dependent on material possessions; wallets full of credit cards all up to their limit.

In one sense there is nothing new in all of this – 'the love of money is the root of all evil' was probably received wisdom long before it was set down in the Bible – but it seems O'Neill is right to think that affluenza could soon reach epidemic proportions in the consumerist West. In a recent questionnaire of American schoolchildren, 93% of teenage girls listed shopping as their favourite pastime. My own research has spotted another possible early sign: it is the relief shown by people who haven't won the lottery when they realise that the jackpot is to be split several ways. After all, what is the point of only winning £400,000?

O'Neill's book itself is also a significant marker: it is easy enough to ignore the pathetic attempts of the May Day marchers to 'denounce capitalism', but when the rich start flogging each other self-help books on how to cope with the destructive power of wealth, it is perhaps time to take notice. (Incidentally, the book is available in hardback, at $20. I sincerely hope that there is a very large pile of them at a certain bookshop in South Kensington.)

*Nick Parker*

# Alternative History

*aka* Da Vinci Code syndrome

In today's high-street bookshop, sitting between the lives of Hitler and the section called 'Mind, Body, Spirit', you can now find another category – 'Alternative History'. The prime volume of Alternative History is *The Tomb of God: The Body of Jesus and the Solution to a 2,000-year-old Mystery*. The claim of the book, by Richard Andrews and Paul Schellenburger, is that Jesus died but did not rise again, and was instead buried in Gaul, at the village of Rennes-le-Château. Haven't we heard that name somewhere else?

Yes indeed, for the mother of all Alternative History books is *Holy Blood, Holy Grail* by Michael Baigent, Richard Leigh and Henry Lincoln (Alternative Historians often feed in packs), first published in 1982.

The story went that Jesus had a child by Mary Magdalene and their progeny later became Merovingian Kings of France, a secret which was kept by the Knights Templars. Then a clandestine set-up called the Priory of Sion, variously headed by Leonardo da Vinci, Isaac Newton and Jean Cocteau, took up the secret, and some priest in the nineteenth century at Rennes-le-Château found out and became very rich.

All this re-emerges in Dan Brown's *The Da Vinci Code* (2003), which takes Alternative History to crazier heights of profitability. Yet, instead of being grateful to the novelist for paradoxically making readers accept their own fiction as fact, the authors of *Holy Blood* seem not to be pleased. They recently sued Mr Brown for 'breach of copyright'. (They lost.)

Airport bookshops are full of Alternative History variants: *The Templar Revelation*; *The Messianic Legacy*; *The Second Messiah*; *Mary Magdalen and the Holy Grail*. In them, Rennes-le-Château, a village fifty miles from Carcassonne, keeps cropping up, and has become a place of Alternative Pilgrimage. An inscription in the church there, *Terribilis est Locus Iste*, is said to mean, 'This place is terrible' – a cryptic indication of its importance in Alternative History. In reality it is a popular quotation from the Bible (Genesis 28:17: 'How dreadful is this place. This is none other but the house of God, and this is the gate of heaven'), which refers to Jacob meeting God.

All this Alternative History goes back, not to the Middle Ages, but to 1956, when the French fantasist Pierre Plantard (1920–2000) became the self-styled Grand Master of the concocted Priory of Sion. Plantard, convicted of financial fraud in 1953, had in 1942 invented another order of chivalry called Alpha Galates. In 1943 he even accused the Vichy regime of being in league with French Jews. From 1962 onwards he invented links between himself and Merovingian kings of France, as well as the other usual suspects.

This Alternative History game of Chinese whispers provoked 150,000 tourists last summer to descend on the little village of Rennes, some carrying spades for a spot of Alternative Archaeology and treasure-hunting: the Abbé Saunière of Rennes-le-Château is said to have suddenly become rich in the 1880s – perhaps by stumbling across buried treasure or by finding parchments that 'proved' Jesus's affair with Mary Magdalene, and enabled him to 'blackmail the Vatican'.

The story of parchments and buried treasure can be traced as far back as 1955 when a local restaurateur who owned a property that was once Saunière's was looking for publicity. A document written by a friend of Plantard's, supposedly transcribing the parchments, was deposited in the Bibliothèque Nationale in 1964. A fact sometimes educed in support of its reliability.

The truth seems to be that Saunière made a few thousand francs by accepting money for Masses that he never said and was suspended from the priesthood as a consequence. However, the books documenting this are in French, and therefore unreadable to most of the US market. They prefer Alternative History.

*Christopher Howse*

**Modern tongue**

## Telephone tirades, No 1

- **'Please hold the line. Your call is important to us'**
  (Although not actually important enough for us to want to speak to you. So please keep holding . . .)
- **'Thank you for your patience'**
  (I'm not being patient, I'm screaming – it's just that no one can hear me because I'm still on hold . . .)

## Ambient

'Ambient' is a marketing term much loved of the music industry. It gets slapped on any musical genre: ambient jazz, ambient classics, ambient world, ambient acid house . . . The music industry loves new categories, as it means another excuse to churn out the same old compilation albums with different sleeves on. It also loves 'ambient' because you can take a genre of music which might be deemed to be 'complicated' or 'difficult' – such as classical or jazz – and by simply adding the prefix 'ambient', you have an excuse to dish out the kind of ersatz slop that would have any genuine music fan gnashing their teeth with rage. Never mind, it'll go nicely with your scented candles. There was never much call for Ambient Mahler anyway.

All music is really ambient, of course – at least it has to get far enough around us to get in at the holes in the sides of our heads. But as a musical term it was first popularised by Brian Eno in the early eighties. Eno, a boffinish dilettante composer who can just about be accommodated by a very baggy use of 'pop', released albums with names such as *Music for Airports* and *Music for Films*, which helped define the nature of 'ambient'. Unlike the bulk of popular chart music nowadays, which comprises almost unadulterated rhythm generated by computers, Eno's synthesisers produced nothing but harmony – rhythm and melody were banished – and varying texture of sound, namely different degrees of burble.

How very boring, you may say, and you would be right. But Eno's rationale was that the music was supposed to be boring, to sink into the background like aural wallpaper. Ah – now we know where we are, you say: ambient is really just old-fashioned muzak. It didn't take someone with a science-fictional name like Eno to think that one up. (Brian's father, incidentally, and unlikely as it may seem, really is Mr Eno, a music teacher from Ipswich.)

Hasn't it always been that way? Wasn't the work of court musicians like Haydn and Mozart just sophisticated background music? I doubt it somehow. Would Prince Esterhazy have spent good money hiring a man like Haydn (and orchestra), only to talk through his performances? Music was one adornment among many, but when it was called for it's probably safe to assume that it was probably listened to. It expressed the ideals of the court, its sense of itself, its structure, its relation to the country.

The idea of ambient removes us further from music as an expression of what we cannot say and relegates it to something that won't interrupt what we do say – as though there wasn't enough chatter in the world.

*Martin Gibson*

## BASE Jumping

BASE jumping is a sport. But unlike, say, cricket, which ideally involves long afternoons on village greens, the gentle crack of leather on willow and warm beer, the ideal BASE jump requires strapping on a high-performance parachute, flinging yourself off something tall and hoping the chute opens before you hit the ground. Each jump lasts about six seconds, and is reputed to give one of the most acute adrenalin rushes it is possible to achieve – except perhaps for that experienced by flinging yourself off a tall building with the intention of committing suicide and accidentally not killing yourself. When you land (assuming that you haven't been paralysed with fear by the experience of 'groundrush', and have failed to open your parachute) you will not be greeted by the ripple of polite applause from the pavilion, but more often by the wail of police sirens, because in most places the sport of BASE jumping is illegal.

BASE jumping began in the early eighties, when skydivers in search of new challenges were hypnotised by a witch into wondering what would happen if they tried opening their chutes below the 2,000 feet at which they would normally pull their rip-cords. BASE is an acronym for Bridge, Antenna, Structure, Earth – the four categories of objects that BASE jumpers leap from, and you are not considered to be a fully-fledged BASE jumper until you have leapt off them all. Bridges are the least problematical as there is no sheer wall to collide with. Buildings have been the most notorious, as some BASE jumpers have flung themselves from high-profile buildings such as the Eiffel Tower and the World Trade Center, a practice which has helped to feed the image of BASE jumpers as reckless adrenalin junkies, law-breakers and attention-seekers. And although many BASE jumpers stick to performing legal, organised jumps with the emphasis on safety and using specially developed equipment and procedures (you are advised to have performed over 200 skydives before attempting your first BASE jump), with a mortality rate of one death every thousand or so jumps it is a reputation they may find difficult to shake. One BASE jumping website carries this enlightening thought: 'There are very few injuries in BASE jumping. Mostly you live, or you die.'

BASE jumping is, you will not be shocked to learn, classed as an 'extreme sport', and these sports have become enormously popular over the last decade. Where once people were happy to spend Bank Holidays paddling in the sea at Clacton, now they don't feel as though they have had a proper break unless they have kayaked over Niagara Falls, snowboarded down K2 or trekked into the mouth of a live volcano. Images of such extreme activities abound in popular culture – if the advertisements are to believed, the only way to enjoy a bottle of pop these days is to drink it while bungee jumping from a helicopter. Extreme sports have also had a profound influence on yoof fashion: your average self-respecting youngster wouldn't dream of setting out for the bus stop without being clad in fast-wicking Gore-Tex fabrics, Polartec insulating fleeces and trousers so hi-tech that with the tug of a Velcro strap they transform into a pair of trekking shorts, a bivouac, or an entire mountaineering base camp.

Psychologists have had a field day. Those of them who are not off BASE jumping have been busy telling us about how this yearning for 'experience' is an attempt to inject a little danger back into our increasingly cosseted Western lives. (I was recently in a building that had a sign saying 'In the interests of safety, patrons are requested to always use the handrail when descending the stairs.' I was strapping on a parachute and halfway to the roof before I came to my senses.) We have not yet learned to cope with the dullness that safety and prosperity can bring. And even though much of the 'extreme' sports scene is not much more than adventure voyeurism (crossing a street at rush hour is more likely to get you injured than a well-organised rafting trip), some sports, such as BASE jumping, are probably destined to remain the province of the genuinely extreme.

Not as extreme as scaling Everest without oxygen, using only hemp ropes and clad in plus-fours, as George Mallory did, mind you . . .

*Nick Parker*

# Bling-bling

'Check out the bling-bling on that!' my twelve-year-old nephew Dante gasped as the Lord Mayor swished past. Dante was, of course, referring to the Lord Mayor's chain. It was big. It glittered. It was fake gold. Yes, it was genuine 24-carat bling-bling. 'Oh my days! Get me one of them things like what that old geezer's got!' Dante demanded. 'Get one for yourself,' I retorted. 'They're only £3.99 at Poundstretcher in Harlesden.'

These days, it's not only Dante who harbours an infernal desire for bling-bling. Everyone under twenty-one knows that bling is the thing. Rap stars from Snoop Doggy Dogg to Li'l Bow Wow continually bark out the order, 'Get blinged or die tryin'.' Gangstas of fashion are bowed down by the weight of jewellery, and when the light catches the fake gems weak eyes cry out for sunglasses. London is ablaze with bling. The necklaces swinging from the chests of today's hipsters make the Lord Mayor's look risibly puny.

Students of blingology will know it was neither Snoop Doggy Dogg nor Li'l Bow Wow who first blinged their way to glory. A hundred years ago in New Orleans, Jelly Roll Morton, the self-styled inventor of jazz, seduced the world with his diamond-studded teeth. His smile purportedly caused as great a sensation as his musical genius. His fellow-artistes, such as Bessie Smith, the Empress of the Blues, knew the wisdom of investing in spectacular bling-bling. Black audiences paid to be dazzled.

However, Bessie's flaunting extravagance occasionally disconcerted her white townsfolk. In 1925, the wife of La Smith's record producer lamented, 'That nigra woman! All them diamonds in her hair, rubies at her throat and a mink coat which posolutely trails on the ground! Seems she done turned too uppity for her own safety!' The Empress, in other words, was bling-blinging in an age when she should have been cringe-cringeing. Her grandmother would have worn a slave collar; sixty years later Bessie sported a diamond choker. Which brings us to the roots of bling.

Bling's source can be neatly traced to the possible ancestors of Jelly, Bessie and Snoopy – the Yoruba peoples of Nigeria. No one in the world can out-bling a Yoruba. Indian saris can just about match Nigerian fabrics glitter for glitter; but the Yoruba physique is just so much beefier than anyone else's that non-Yorubas inevitably appear colourless in comparison. Yorubas don't waste their nairas on adding gob-ons to their houses, going on expensive holidays or even buying flashy electrical gadgets. They beautify themselves. Every Yoruba man and woman is a walking work of art. Hand-woven shimmering material around the waist and cloth of gold balanced alarmingly on the head creates an effect equalled only by Chaucer's Wife of Bath, whose 'handkerchieven weighed her to the ground'.

Perhaps the most spectacular Yoruba adornments are the elaborately plaited hairstyles, which can take five whole days to complete. In a land where slavery is openly practised, it is very disconcerting for the dowdy foreigner to be served by a house-girl who blazes like the Queen of Sheba in all her magnificence.

And now the descendants of these human pageants have colonised the world with their music and bling-bling. All over Europe, India, China, Japan, Russia – even in communist Laos, style warriors are blinging it on down to the beat of Afro-America. Whatever their original language, no youngster in the world is unable to translate this phrase.

Yo! Ho! Fo, shizzle I sing,
If you ain't got bling-bling
You ain't got nothin' there,
In fact, you ain't nowhere.

*Zenga Longmore*

*'We no longer tell people to lie back and think of England. You should lie back and celebrate Britishness.'*

# Blog

A blog, gentle reader, is cyber-nerd slang for a 'weblog', and that, GR, is a diary-style website where some poor soul ('blogger') has posted up his or her diary, list of prejudices, stream of consciousness, or whatever is on their minds. Blogs will often contain links to other websites that the blogger has enjoyed. Frequently these will be other blogs. A blog is not the same as a biog, though many are autobiographical, and blogging isn't the same as blagging, though it can have some of the same flavour. You can blag in a blog.

Some people maintain that blogging is the last great step in the democratisation of information. At last! Everyone has a voice! I can instantly access the opinions of someone on the other side of the world. We can communicate directly without 'interference' from 'the media'. There is some truth in this – during the Iraq war, a number of Iraqis kept blogs, giving insights into what was really going on in Baghdad.

By and large, though, it turns out that wherever you live, the chances are that if you have a blog you'll write the same kind of pointless, self-regarding drivel as anyone else. You'll say what records you're listening to, what things you think are cool, what other things you think are dumb, and you'll link to a couple of news articles on the BBC website. If we're lucky, you might be witty. Chances are you'll be extremely dull. It turns out that 'media interference' also largely equates to 'quality control' and 'access to a decent editor'.

Figures suggest that the 'blogosphere' has doubled in size every five months over the past three years, so that the total number or weblogs now in existence is around 19.6 million, churning out tens of millions of pages of commentary a year. Last year, the first blogging collection was published in book form. That's several million pages distilled into one single 256-page paperback. Nuff said.

*Caroline Richmond*

## Bluetooth

The words 'bluetooth technology' are now as common, and about as annoying, as the words 'Railtrack' and 'delays'. And none of us has the foggiest what they mean. But it's not just another techie widget, this time it's important. You're going to need to know. So you might as well get it over and done with now.

Bluetooth is an open specification short-wave radio technology that allows voice and digital data connections to be made over distances up to ten metres. What this means to you and me is that all your bits of technology which now have to be connected to each other by cables will be able to communicate with each other via wireless connections. More significantly, all your other bits of technology which were previously content to sit around doing nothing much, such as your toaster and your fridge, will suddenly become 'live'. Bluetooth technology is cheap, so even the most basic appliances will come fitted with a chip, and because it is 'open specification', all different makes and brands will be compatible with each other.

The possibilities for bluetooth are endless. You will be able to make your telly talk to your microwave so that your tea is ready exactly when *Eastenders* finishes. Your fridge will be able to tell when you run out of milk, and it will be able to communicate this to your car, which will remind you on the way home from work that you need to pop to the shops. You will be able to use your mobile phone like an *über*-remote control, using it to open your curtains, boil the kettle and turn on your house alarm when you leave. If you have a computer in your home with a bluetooth connection, it will be possible to send emails home from your desk at work, to tell the computer to set the video, turn on the heating, probably even let the cat out.

As I'm sure you're fast coming to realise, bluetooth is going to be a nightmare. As a measure of just how colossally awful things could well turn out to be, think about this: it will be possible, in the very near future, to be sitting on a train next to a man barking into his mobile phone to 'put a brew on, I'll be home in five minutes' – *and he could be talking to his own kettle.*

This is not just my own techno-paranoia. In the USA, there are bluetooth communities doing trials with this revolutionary technology. These are some of the calls that they have logged with the Bluetooth Helpline:

- A user called to say that he suspected that his fridge was ordering extra milk for his cat, without telling him.
- A man was nearly driven insane when his bluetooth kettle was accidentally fitted with a tamagotchi chip. He had to drink at least fifteen cups of tea a day, or his kettle would cause a big emotional scene every time he had visitors.
- A woman phoned her microwave to tell it to heat up her ready-meal as she was just turning into her street. Her microwave said that she ate quite enough junk food already, and hadn't she really oughta watch her diet, what with those thighs?

And this is just the thin end of the wedge. Just imagine what might happen if your entire bluetooth network got a computer virus. You could return from work one day and find your house filled with milk, and your toaster and your kettle sitting on the sofa watching early episodes of *Frazier* and emailing out for pizza. Bluetooth will promise us the earth, then bugger everything up. Throw away your remote controls now. You have been warned.

*Nick Parker*

# Boxfresh

Thirty years ago, trainers were objects of derision, if not pity. Inelegant and clumpish, frowned upon by gym masters, and used for football only when your boots were in a state of savage disrepair, they were the shoe world's last resort. Being seen in public in trainers would have incited general condemnation, possibly even arrest. If you felt the urge to don footwear made of rubber, there was always the plimsoll. Even in the eighties and early nineties, the first thing you did when you bought a pair of trainers was scuff them up a bit. Your first outing in them would inevitably be traumatic – strangers would point and laugh at your Bright White Trainers. More and more people might be wearing them, but we didn't like to be reminded of the fact that we'd bought them out of choice. We had the good grace to be embarrassed.

Now the plimsoll is dead and the war is lost. There is no shame any more in owning a pair of trainers. Everyone between the ages of two and two hundred will have at least two pairs by the front door. They embody the holy grail of modern life: youth, fitness and comfort. We are no longer squeamish about the bright plasticky shamelessness of a brand new training shoe. In fact, we revel in it. Ah, the smell of the petrochemicals. The crinkle of the tissue paper wrapping against the 100 per cent synthetic uppers. Regard the unsullied injection-moulded sole. Admire the stitching around the corporate logo. This pristine state is 'boxfresh'.

There was a time when goods were made to get better with age, to be shaped by the passing of time and the love of their owners: a sturdy leather bag, a trusty corduroy jacket, a fountain pen that would shape itself around your handwriting or a cricket bat that would carry the memories of every crack of the ball. Boxfresh laughs in the face of such sentimentality. Boxfresh means that like rap mogul Damon Dash, only by chucking your new trainers away after you've worn them once and replacing them with a new pair can you reach Training Shoe Nirvana. Boxfresh is a kind of parody of the subtle pleasures of ownership. Fresh! Ha! Like they were some kind of organic vegetable, or like an oyster teased from its shell.

It's insanity. The Campaign for Real Plimsolls starts here.

*Marcus Berkmann*

*'If you're happy and you know it, clap your hands.'*

## Brainstorming

It is a truth universally acknowledged that business managers love buzzwords. They are constantly pushing envelopes, running things up flagpoles (to see how they flutter) and engaging in blue-sky thinking. Buzzwords usually contain no information that couldn't be communicated more effectively in normal language, but that, of course, would be defeating the whole object of the exercise: buzzwords are meant to be exclusive, to make the user sound dynamic, up-to-the-minute, and capable of drilling down to find a strategic fit for any mission-critical future-proofing that might need doing. I'm sure you know what I mean.

The grandfather of all buzzwords is 'brainstorming', which now sounds faintly old fashioned, but is very much alive and well and causing untold havoc in the business world. I used to work at a company where everything was 'brainstormed'. New idea for a slogan? Let's brainstorm it. What colour should the box be? Let's have a colour brainstorm. What biscuits does everybody want with elevenses? Time for a hob-nob brainstorm. One colleague heading for the loo could often be heard muttering, 'Just off for a brainstorm . . .'

The irony is that brainstorming, far from being just another meaningless buzzword, is a concept with a rather more distinguished pedigree. It was the, er, brainchild of American advertising executive Alex F. Osborn. Ever since the day a newspaper editor told Osborn in 1915 that he liked his pieces because each one 'contained an idea', Osborn had been obsessed with the notion of the creative process.

By 1941 he had turned creative thinking into a lucrative career and was running a successful advertising agency. But he was finding that traditional business meetings did not work well for generating creative ideas: younger executives would inevitably feel inhibited by more senior colleagues, and most people were reluctant to say things that might sound 'wrong' or 'stupid'. To counteract this, Osborn proposed some rules for these meetings. He initially called this process 'thinking up', but the meetings soon became known as 'brainstorming sessions' because participants saw the approach almost as the military bombardment of a problem.

Osborn's brainstorming rules were as follows: no criticism of ideas (judgements can be made later); aim for large quantities of ideas; encourage wild and exaggerated ideas (it is 'easier to tame down than to think up'); and build on each other's ideas. The key rule, Osborn maintained, was the first one: 'If you try to get hot and cold water out of the same faucet at the same time, you will get only tepid water. And if you try to criticise and create at the same time, you can't turn on either the cold enough criticism or the hot enough ideas.'

Osborn built on his concept over the years, and in 1953 published *Applied Imagination*, which contained explanations and refinements of brainstorming, as well as much passionate extolling of the virtues of creative thinking in general: 'We need new ideas to win wars. We need even more and better new ideas to win peace.' It's a shame that this principle doesn't lie behind the majority of contemporary buzzwords. Perhaps a brainstorming session is required to address this problem?

NB: Readers wanting to practise a bit of brainstorming might like to use the following Osborn exercise: 'If an aspiring politician wanted to stand out sartorially, what three ideas might you suggest along the lines of Chamberlain's umbrella?'

*Nick Parker*

## Call Centres

Here's the thing. I wrote the original article on 'What is a Call Centre?' just five years ago. At the time, the idea that you could innocently call your bank branch to speak to your bank manager, only to find that your call had been re-routed to a large tin shed on the outskirts of Glasgow, where it would be answered by a clueless 'operative' reading their responses off a multiple choice list on computer screen, *and that this state of affairs was deemed by the banks to be an improvement*, seemed baffling and preposterous. Some *Oldie* readers wrote to us in shock and amazement. They had been wondering why calling their banks had become such a trying experience of late.

And here we are five years later and I've had to scrap the original piece. It was about as enlightening as if I'd written explaining 'What is decimalisation?' We all now instinctively understand that when we pick up the phone to talk to any organisation larger than a corner shop, the chances are we'll get a call centre instead. We understand how to conduct a three-way conversation between ourselves, the clueless operative, and the computer terminal who is really in charge. Complaining about this state of affairs is now as irrelevant as complaining that we have to work for a living. It's life. We get on with it. The very idea that there was ever a time that one would have been allowed to simply pick up the telephone and speak to one's *actual bank manager* is now the thing that seems baffling and preposterous. The manager? Of the bank? Were we mad? We shudder at our own naivete.

But of course that hasn't been the end of it. Nowadays the chances are that when we pick up the telephone and dial an organisation, our calls are being answered by call centres in *India*. India now employs 350,000 people in the call centre industry, almost all of them offering 'back office' support to European and American companies. And already, the idea of ringing your bank on the high street and being put through to a call centre *on the other side of the fucking planet, in a wholly different time zone, and utterly alien culture*, doesn't seem that weird. It doesn't seem that weird that they're working a night shift in order to talk to us during the day. It doesn't seem that weird that the person in India says things like 'Are you going to be watching the big game on Saturday?' – because we know they are given regular 'local information' updates in which they are taught to say such things. It doesn't seem weird that we can be haranguing someone about raising our overdraft limit by £500, while at the same time knowing in the backs of our minds that they're probably earning a dollar a day. It doesn't seem weird that when I slam the phone down on a cold caller with a Bangalore accent asking if I'd be interested in uPVC windows, I have to deal with an unsettling frisson of imperialist guilt.

If you throw a bunch of frogs into a pot of boiling water, they'll leap straight out. If you put them in a pot of cold water then gradually turn up the heat, they'll happily sit there while they boil to death.

Press 1 if you feel something is going terribly awry.

*Nick Parker*

**Modern tongue**

## Telephone tirades, No 2

- **'Your call may be monitored for security reasons'**
  (What security reasons?)
- **'Your call may be monitored for staff training purposes'**
  (Wait, I thought you were monitoring for security reasons?)

# Chavs

As I wait my turn to be served in a shop, I catch sight of a girl in her late teens at the front of the queue, wearing velour tracksuit bottoms sagging below her waistline, a tight vest, chunky gold ear-rings and a baseball cap tipped at a jaunty angle over her ponytail. We aren't in Brooklyn, however, but Croydon, where this form of attire is proudly flaunted by a social group mockingly labelled 'chavs'.

To Scots they're known as 'neds', to Liverpudlians they're 'scallies'. Add to the list 'pikeys', 'janners', 'kevs', 'steeks', 'spides', 'charvers', 'bazzas', 'yarcos', 'ratboys', 'Kappa slappers', 'skangers', 'scutters', 'stigs', 'hood rats', and we have a wide variety of names stretching from one end of the country to the other. Yet their meaning remains unanimous. 'Chav' is slang for a person of working-class origin, generally poorly educated and often casually dressed in sportswear. The Scottish variant is supposedly an acronym of 'non-educated delinquents', but whatever term is used, it is always derogatory.

'Britain's peasant underclass are taking over our towns and cities,' according to chavscum.co.uk, which humorously examines the rise of the country's new ruling class. David and Victoria Beckham are 'celebrity chavs', alongside footballer Wayne Rooney and glamour model Jordan. The site offers guidance on 'how to spot a chav' and features a 'chav of the month', as well as a forum for discussing the chav way of life. Decked from head to toe in fashionable brands adorned with logos, the ubiquitous baseball cap (often in a poor imitation of the Burberry check), white trainers and flashy jewellery, chavs present an image described as 'council-estate chic', as opposed to the American equivalent, 'trailer-park trash'.

Other forms of youth subculture have been defined by popular music, be they mods, rockers, punks or teddy boys, and the chav movement is no different, with its participants adapting the style evoked by American hip-hop. The Streets' Mike Skinner is applauded for his skill in portraying British urban street culture in chav lingo. An example is the song 'Fit But You Know It' ('fit' being the parlance for someone who is good-looking).

While The Streets are taken seriously by pundits and music fans, a hip-hop collective by the name of Goldie Lookin' Chain (spot the irony?) has emerged from Newport, South Wales, kitted out in cheap leisure wear and 'bling-bling', rapping about white suburban life and name-dropping Argos, a chain allegedly favoured by this urban tribe for its tacky sovereign rings, big hoop earrings and thick gold chains. Chavs may be mocked, but many are jumping on the bandwagon and exploiting their values.

It is thought the word chav derives from the name of the town of Chatham in Kent. However, its roots belong to gypsies, as the word 'chavvi', which comes from the Romany for male child, or 'chavvo' as the feminine noun, has been part of their language for generations. Its current use, however, has very little connection with its origins.

Chavs are currently blamed for just about all antisocial behaviour, the rise in teenage pregnancy, being obese, dumbed-down television, perverting the aspirations of the whole of the working class, calling their kids things like 'Tequila', making town centres unsafe at night and, presumably, the stagnation of the housing market and the increasing threat of global warming. It'll all be over soon and someone else will be to blame. But for now, chav is the new black.

*Afsheen Shaikh*

## Chick Lit

The heroine, typically, is Joanne. She has a job in publicity. Or marketing. Or she is assistant to someone in TV, a sub on a magazine, a drama student – it hardly impinges, she never stays long. The same with men. She tries them out, finds them wanting, wants something better. She is insecure, expectant, fearful of getting pregnant. But marriage, though she won't admit it, is her ambition. Dissatisfaction hovers over her and to dispel it she gets pissed, which gives her a hangover, which leaves her doubly dissatisfied. She lives for what might happen after work tonight, at the weekend, on holiday. And what happens is predictable.

On page one she wakes up in bed. Is it her own? If not,

whose? How she got there is a blur, and she can't identify the body beside her. Three hundred pages later she is in bed again, with the right man at last. On the way she has clubbed and pubbed, spent hours on the phone, told lies to people she loves, ridden in sports cars belonging to men mostly called Alex and in a stretch limo to an awful hen party. Every fifty pages she weeps another bucketful. The reader stays dry-eyed, with a sort of numb admiration for such exuberance.

Joanne's interests are calories, knickers, aftershave, signs of the zodiac, a ticket for the rugby at Twickers and plenty of testosterone with Chardonnay to go with it. She doesn't make love so much as 'do it' in a haze of alcohol, or she grabs a quickie on the stairs at a party. Foreplay consists of pages of dialogue in a breathless girlie tone and lots *of arrrgggh, bleurgh, phwoar, cwah-cwah* and *unh-huh* to fill the gaps. In book after book she drops the same names – film stars, pop stars, footballers, DJs, ephemeral celebs, with dollops of Diana, Charles and Camilla. Or sometimes Richard Branson. She's jealous of anyone who gets into *Hello!* and can reach peaks of bitchiness towards her best friends. Relationships are what makes the world go round, but in the end she finds that sex is sex is sex.

That's Chick Lit in an eggshell.

*Nicholas Wollaston*

# Chickenability

Walter Pater wrote that 'all art constantly aspires to the condition of music'. In the food industry, it would seem that all groceries constantly aspire to the condition of chicken. All food manufacturers know that chicken is the touchstone of foodstuffs. So much so that in 2001 the marketing team charged with relaunching a popular British brand came up with the notion of 'chickenability'. The idea was that non-poultry food products could be marketed to represent the convenience and familiarity of chicken.

After a company merger, Young's Bluecrest, the largest producer of seafood in the UK, decided to focus their relaunch campaign on giving their fish products 'chickenability'. They realised that although consumers liked eating fish, they were put off by the attendant skin and bones. They therefore set about developing fish products which offered the accessibility and convenience of a cellophane-wrapped chicken breast, taking away all the 'nasties'.

The desirability of chicken rests on its familiarity and affordability. It is also a meat acceptable to most religions and cultures. As a white meat, chicken is the meat of choice for the health-conscious, and it accounts for nearly half of all fresh meat eaten in the UK. According to research by the European Commission, chicken is the 'meat of the future', and consumption is predicted to rise from the 21 kg consumed per capita in 2000 to 24.8 kg in

2008. Not good news if you're a battery chicken.

The rise of chicken poses a huge challenge to those products that aspire to chickenability. Can other foodstuffs ever win the accolade of 'the new chicken'? Or, as the *Grocer* magazine put it last year, 'Can salmon become the new poultry?' Will brainwashed consumers one day find themselves slipping microwaveable sushi-flavoured potato fingers into their shopping baskets with the easy familiarity of a pack of chicken drumsticks? And what about the vegetarians? According to the Vegetarian Society, 5 per cent of the UK's adult population is vegetarian and this increases by an average of 2,000 people a week. Perhaps the world is ready for the next stage: courgettability.

The drive to supply the consumer's insatiable appetite for chicken is neatly satirised in Margaret Atwood's recent novel, *Oryx and Crake,* set in the near future of genetic engineering. Her fictional food scientists have developed an organism which they have affectionately dubbed 'chickienobs'. These are genetically altered chickens that have no feathers and no brains and produce only the most useful chicken parts, such as legs and breasts. This endlessly replenishing flesh can be sliced off in the manner of a doner kebab. Perhaps this is the ultimate in 'chickenability' – the boneless, skinless, eternally renewing convenience meal.

The very inoffensiveness of chicken (inoffensive, that is, if you're not a vegetarian or a Buddhist) has a lot to answer for. Have you noticed that whenever someone tries to persuade you to sample something ostensibly unappetising – be it frogs' legs or pigs' testicles – they always use the line that 'it tastes just like chicken'? There was a story in the papers recently about a woman from Brighton who placed an advertisement for her placenta in the window of a vegetarian food shop. Her reasoning was that it would be a pity for such a nutritious piece of meat to go to waste. 'Fried with a little garlic and some oregano, it's delicious,' the woman claimed. 'A bit like chicken, actually.'

*Emma Harding*

*'He still refuses to upgrade.'*

## Colonics

There is an engaging battiness about the outer reaches of alternative medicine. Reiki, for example, is based on ancient Tibetan knowledge and 'attunes an individual to being a receiver for Universal Life Energy Vibration'. While with Tragerwork, 'the practitioner tries to create a safe non-judgemental experience reminiscent of when we were babies cradled in our mother's arms'. The curious thing about these and other fringe therapies – reflexology, iridology, aromatherapy, shamanism and rolfing, to mention a few – is that they are so innocuous. The practitioner passes his hands over the usually recumbent body of his 'client', shines a light in his eyes, manipulates the bones in his feet or rubs oil into his back and thighs, but not a lot happens.

The same cannot be said for colonic lavage, also known as colonic irrigation, colonic hydrotherapy or, to the initiated, just 'colonics'. Transfixed by a plastic tube up the rectum with ten gallons of warm water splashing around in the colon, the client can have little doubt that he (or, more usually, she) is getting his/her money's worth.

First, there is the smell let loose by many years' worth of encrusted faeces being washed out. 'It's like turning over ripe compost,' according to Nancy Gardener, President of the California Colonic Hygienists Society.

Then there is the moment of catharsis, eloquently described by the arch priestess of fringe medicine, Kristin Olsen:

'I experienced a tremendous release of materials. It felt like a sudden liberation of energy that had literally been captured in my intestines all this time. I shook as it was released and shed the tears I was not allowed to show. It was a cleansing crisis.'

After years of unjustified neglect, colonics are now very much back in fashion – their acceptance in polite society prompted, no doubt, by rumours that the late Princess of Wales was such a keen user she practically had a bucket with her own name on.

Colonic irrigation was first practised by the ancient Egyptians, who borrowed the idea from the sacred Ibis. His unusual eliminative habits involved sucking seawater up into his beak and then syringing the contents into his anus. As Herodotus of Halicarnassus observed: 'Egyptians purge themselves every month on three successive days, for they suppose that all diseases to which man is subject proceed from the food they use.'

Medieval physicians were great enthusiasts for no better reason than that irrigation was one of the few remedies prescribed that palpably worked and seemed less injurious than the alternative of bleeding.

Colonic irrigation peaked in popularity in France in the late sixteenth century. Louis XIII had 213 lavages in one year and his son reputedly had 2,000 over his lifetime. The complex courtly ritual required first that the king's medical advisers manoeuvre him into the right position on the side of the bed; they would then stand aside for the apothecary carrying the cannula in his hand, who was followed by his apprentice carrying the syringe; bringing up the rear (as it were) of the procession was another boy with a light to illuminate the scene. With such royal endorsement, the craze for colonics swept Parisian society, some women managing to fit in three or four a day, motivated mostly by the strong belief that they improved the complexion.

The subsequent neglect of colonics was due to the discovery of purgative pills, which achieved with less bother and more decorum the same effect.

Science, in the form of the microscope, restored their reputation. The bowel, it appeared, was literally teeming with hundreds of millions of bacteria to whose toxins could plausibly enough be attributed virtually any disease or state of chronic ill health. This theory of 'auto-intoxication' inspired the imagination of many eminent physicians, including Dr William Kerr Russell, whose book, *Colonic Irrigation*, published in the 1930s, provides the clearest rationale for the use of colonics in the scientific age. 'The penalties of neglecting the human drainage system are immeasurable,' he wrote. 'It must be obvious that chronic stagnation of the bowels must lead to chronic poisoning of the whole system.' Colonic irrigation, he maintained, provided the only rational treatment, 'stimulating the bowel to perform its functions by means of colon gymnastics'.

The list of conditions that might be expected to improve with irrigation was a lengthy one: as well as constipation, colic, flatulence and infective diarrhoea, migraine and vertigo, neurasthenia and manic depression, irregularities of the heartbeat, bronchitis and sinusitis, a sallow complexion and psoriasis, haemorrhoids and gallstones were all associated with or exacerbated by abnormalities of bowel functions.

It is easy to mock such enthusiasm, but to be fair to Dr Kerr Russell, there is a most curious association between the state of the bowels and psychological well-being – anxiety notoriously precipitates bouts of diarrhoea; those of nervous disposition frequently suffer from the irritable bowel syndrome; and constipation has many diffuse and apparently unrelated symptoms, including a debilitating lethargy and melancholy.

It would be surprising, then, if colonic irrigation did not have the euphoriant effect that so many surprised customers attribute to it. Journalist Ysenda Maxtone Graham describes it as: 'the most satisfying loo-going experience of my life. Years of stored-up wind and matter, such as old pips, stones and undigested pills, are dispensed with. It is a joy to say goodbye to them.'

Orthodox medicine is unimpressed. According to John Northover, consultant surgeon at St Mark's Hospital in London, and quoted in the *Evening Standard*, 'the idea that it is some form of cure or a way of maintaining good health is just ludicrous, absolute piffle. It is just straightforward quackery'.

This misses the point. No one should take seriously the ability of alternative therapies to cure serious illnesses. Many therapies, including colonic irrigation, do, however, provide a first-rate, feel-good experience – and who is to argue with that?

*James LeFanu*

## Colour-coded Compassion

They are totally unavoidable. Scan any tube carriage, bus or train, and you are guaranteed to see people wearing rubber wristbands in lots of different colours. They are cheap to make and cheap to buy – and yet the wearer is proud to wear one. These ubiquitous pieces of 'jewellery' are colour-coded charity wristbands. They are a fashion phenomenon, the must-have accessory for anyone who thinks they're both trendy and 'aware' of 'global issues' – compassion made stylish.

The craze started in the USA. In 2003, Lance Armstrong, the brilliant Tour de France cyclist who was diagnosed with a virulent cancer, launched the 'Livestrong' campaign. Yellow wristbands with 'Livestrong' imprinted on them were sold for $1, the proceeds going to Lance's cancer charity, the Lance Armstrong Foundation. Suddenly Hollywood was seen wearing them, and quickly the yellow bracelets became an essential fashion item for the American public. The craze spread worldwide. The LAF has sold over ten million wristbands.

Other charities soon followed suit. Breast cancer, HIV,

diabetes, leukaemia, Asperger's – all these diseases and syndromes have their own colour-coded charity wristbands. Marketing and PR bods were also quick to catch on, and the wristband was taken up not only by charities, but by causes, too – blue for Radio One's 'beat bullying' campaign, black and white wristbands worn together for the 'Stand Up and Speak Up' kick racism out of football campaign. And of course the white 'Make Poverty History' wristband which did so much to banish poverty from the planet once and for all. There was much jostling for position among the charities over who claimed which colours: after all, who wants to be left with their cause being championed by a beige wristband?

In schools across the country, pupils would wear many bracelets at once. To much media commotion, some schools started banning the rubber bands, claiming they didn't fit in with the uniform, or worrying that pupils might cheat in their exams by writing on them. Other schools have wholeheartedly embraced wristband culture – on leaving Westminster School last year, sixth formers could buy a pink rubber bracelet with 'Rohan Westminster 2005' imprinted on it. Rohan is the name of the Tsunami relief fund to which the proceeds went. But one can't help feeling that the school was just trying to cash in on this culture of showy compassion.

Wristband culture is an odd thing. In wearing one, the owner must feel a need to publicly proclaim his compassion for a cause and his 'awareness' of the 'issues' (frequently used words in the world of rubber wristbands) that the bracelet signifies – whilst also remaining fashionable. It's the same sort of charity culture that breeds Comic Relief – people making token gestures to a charity to make themselves feel better, and then forgetting about it for the rest of the time.

A final helpful hint – if you must wear one of those yellow 'Livestrong' wristbands, remember to take it off if you go into hospital. They're the same colour as the wristbands used to denote patients with 'do not resuscitate' orders.

*Sonali Chapman*

**Modern tongue**

### Top five irritants

1 'Have a nice day!'
2 'Your call is important to us'
3 'No probs!'
4 'Chill out'
5 'Bear with us'

# Corporate Bonding

Have you ever wondered what fruit you are? Or if you had to be a planet, which one you would be? If you have gone through life without tackling these important questions it is unlikely that you've been on a corporate bonding day.

In order that you get the most out of your corporate bonding day, you first need to find yourself a company who will lay on a ridiculous activity for you all to participate in. Phoenix Leisure, for example, offer car racing, paint-balling, ballooning, treasure hunts or falconry, while Accolade, who claim to 'deal in memories and give memories to your staff', give you the opportunity to make a film and attend an Oscar ceremony, or dress up as knights in armour and fight your colleagues. A typical day may begin with 'personal profiling', where staff are set challenging questions with the aim of team-building and breaking the ice. After a liquid lunch the serious physical stuff begins. There may well be an opportunity to cross a river with the aid of a few random pieces of wood and your entire advertising department, or, if you are really lucky, to dress up as a cowboy and ride a go-kart herding colleagues dressed as cows. Grappling over obstacle courses with Doreen from Accounts might not be your idea of fun, but you are 'nurturing camaraderie'.

If it all gets too much, you can bolster your flagging morale with tales of corporate bonding sessions that have gone wrong: such as the contingent of Burger King staff in Florida who were burned in a team fire-walking session (perhaps they were being encouraged to *really understand flame-grilling, from the burger's perspective*?).

Or what about when the *Observer* newspaper sent senior staff on a bonding exercise to Minster Lovell in Oxfordshire. Section editors were gelling happily until Tuesday night, when the newspaper laid on free drinks in the bar. Frank Kane, the business editor, became increasingly friendly with his colleagues, eventually bursting into his canon of Irish rebel songs – which so offended Andy Malone, the home news editor, that he lashed out. Kane was felled with a single punch. 'We were experimenting with anger management techniques,' said Malone.

The thinking behind corporate bonding seems to be that a more integrated staff makes a happier staff, and a happier staff is a more productive staff. Unfortunately, this thinking may be all wrong: According to a recent BBC report, unhappy people make the best workers. Cheerful workers waste too much time, while the dour ones get on with the task.

Or perhaps managing directors secretly know this: It's not that they desperately hope corporate bonding days will bring us together as one big happy smiling adversity-facing family, but that they know being forced to attend one will make us even more miserable than before, so we'll knuckle down and clear that in-tray. Perhaps, after all, we are all bananas.

*Ben Tisdall*

## Creative Play

Whatever happened to the joyful aimlessness of childhood? Of lazy days spent stamping on ants, playing knock-down ginger and pinching apples from next door's tree? And then there were acts of random yet satisfying violence against siblings. At the age of three, my still dear brother shut my head in the fridge door. It didn't half hurt at the time, but at least I can now value its spontaneity. 'Creative play', on the other hand, is about as spontaneous as the closing speech at a Labour Party conference.

This expression, which originated in the USA, is now bandied about over here by health clinics, nursery schools and anyone else wishing to appear educationally progressive. Health visitors are particularly fond of the term. At the two-year check-up, an array of brightly coloured educational toys will be placed in front of your nonchalant child, who will then be asked to perform a series of boring tasks with them. Invariably, he or she will refuse to participate, preferring instead to rifle through the health visitor's handbag in search of something more interesting to play with (usually tampons). 'Mum,' the health visitor will eventually ask, staring in a concerned way at your offspring, 'do you encourage your child through creative play?'

'Of course!' you cry. 'I have to be the Child Catcher from *Chitty Chitty Bang Bang* and chase her round the house.' However, imagination alone is not enough to convince a third party of a child's creative potential. Children are now expected to be splendid all-rounders, practically from the moment they leave the womb. If they fail to display exquisite threading, balancing, construction and motor skills by certain set targets, parents are made to feel they have given birth to the village idiot.

And since adults started making such a big deal out of 'creative play', schools need only drop this meaningless expression into their prospectus to have hordes of eager, impressed parents putting little Johnny's name down. 'Creative Play can help a child express himself through such things as drawing, painting, making Play-Doh models, sticking and glueing and cooking,' they state, as if no one had thought of doing these things with our children before they came along and suggested it.

In recent years, toy manufacturers have even leapt on to the 'creative play' bandwagon by turning it into a clever marketing device. Simply put 'Stimulates Creative Play' on any box containing any old toy and the shelves will be emptied within weeks. The toy manufacturer Little Tikes has created seventy new toys under the banner of 'creative play', yet most of them are anything but creative, as they appear to do everything for you. There's the Tender Sounds 'n' Motion Nursery (age 2 to 6), a horrific-sounding contraption described as an 'interactive, electronic nursery that rocks, plays music and makes baby sounds'; or how about Disney's Pooh Play Tree Climber where 'kids can climb Pooh's purple tree house'? What's wrong with climbing real trees? No money in it, I suppose.

A progression from 'creative play' can be witnessed later on in the 'after-school activity'. Here, ambitious parents for whom money is no object book their child in for tennis and swimming lessons, violin lessons, acting lessons, chess, karate, judo and goodness knows what else in order to bring out that child's 'creative energy'.

Those who can't be doing with all this malarky are left vaguely wondering if they are stifling their child's inner genius. My six-year-old son, Fred, who has a strange talent for befriending rich people's children, has a friend who is forever being carted off to one after-school activity or another. When his nanny rings up to ask my son over, Fred – a latter-day Pip – invariably ends up wandering around their huge house on his own, while his friend lies slumped on the sofa, watching telly with his mouth open. 'He's no fun any more,' grumbled Fred after the last visit. Well, would you be after a week of being Yehudi Menuhin, Pete Sampras, Sammy Davis Jr and Bruce Lee all rolled into one? As his Czech nanny once said, 'They work him too hard. He always tired.' Give the child a break. After all, at what other time in his life will he get away with doing absolutely nothing without feeling guilty about it?

*Alice Pitman*

## La Crise

The French have always had a penchant for being existentially sombre or philosophically depressed. And, of course, we know how much they love to voice their discontentment with a good old strike. That said, the French seem more miserable than ever at the moment – so much so that the French media have named the nationwide gloom, which descended on France after the summer holiday in 2005, 'La Crise'.

This nationwide depression is thanks to a number of factors. For a start, the loss of the 2012 Olympic bid. The tabloid newspaper *France Soir* reported at the end of August: 'The French went on holiday with their morale already at rock bottom. They were crushed by the insolent success of the British, their eternal rivals . . .' While we Brits were printing T-shirts reading 'Agincourt, Trafalgar, Waterloo, 2012', the French feeling of self-worth had apparently dropped to nil.

Then in Toronto, an Air France Jumbo Airbus overshot the runway whilst landing in bad weather before bursting into flames. Though no one was killed, this crash – when coupled with the Venezuela plane crash earlier in the year which killed French Caribbeans – caused hysteria among some French holidaymakers who cancelled their trip and refused to fly. The *Times* reported on 30 August that 'hundreds of airline passengers have mutinied in the past two weeks, refusing to board foreign charter aircraft that frightened them'. So not only were they miserable

– they were trapped in France with lots of other miserable French people.

In truth, this decline in public mood has been building up for a number of years now. The French are very proud of being French: they are proud of their heritage, their cooking, their art, their wine, their language – and yet they feel that these things, the very things that make up their 'Frenchness', are slipping away in favour of so-called 'Anglo-Saxon' globalisation. And perhaps they are right. Not even their currency is French any more – the franc, originally re-established as national currency after the revolution in 1795 and thus imbued with connotations of 'Liberté, Egalité, Fraternité', has been replaced by the Euro. France no longer exists in currency – it has merely been amalgamated into one large continent.

And the French language, despite the people's fierce efforts to protect it (especially in Paris, where even if you speak impeccable French they will reply to you only in English), has been invaded by Americanisms and anglicised vocabulary: le weekend, c'est cool, le hamburger, le camping, le sandwich, le cocktail . . . the list goes on.

And perhaps most shocking of all is the closure at the end of August of the last French factory making Gauloise cigarettes. Gauloises, the epitome of Frenchness, once glorified in a duet by Serge Gainsbourg and Catherine Deneuve, smoked by Jean-Paul Sartre and Picasso, are no longer made anywhere in France. Those remaining French who are still loyal to their brand will have to buy their cigarettes imported from a factory in Spain. And what has replaced the French Dark Gauloise, whose packets display the winged helmet of the ancient French Gauls? Why, American tobacco, of course. Said Aneta Lazarevic, spokesperson for the company that manufactures Gauloises: 'We faced a fast-growing overcapacity due to declining sales. Just like all categories of food products, people seem to want a sweeter taste.'

And that sweeter taste is provided by the U S of A. No wonder the French are so depressed. That's like making HP sauce in America. Oh, wait, it may be made near Birmingham, but HP is owned by Heinz . . . Is this the start of our own crisis?

*Sonali Chapman*

*'I'm afraid "Opening Modern Packaging" is fully subscribed.'*

## Customer Care

Companies don't *care about* their customers. They *care that you remain a customer of theirs.*

*Nick Parker*

## Cycleway

A country 'cycleway' is an existing road marked as a 'cycleway', which you had always been able to cycle on before it became a 'cycleway'. Small blue signs at cycling height have started appearing across the counties, but since they point in opposite directions it is difficult to know which way to go if you want to discover where they lead to. They are, according to the 'cycleway' leaflet, designed to encourage people 'to cycle through the glorious countryside and see rural England at its best'. We have had this option ever since bicycles were invented.

In truth, they are designed for the more timid among us who do not know where they want to go until they are told; according to the Highways Department at Trowbridge in Wiltshire, 'a high proportion of the population likes to be nurtured and there is a large demand for this sort of organised leisure'.

Cycleways are only the tip of an enormous signing iceberg. The whole of Britain's countryside is being signed up in an effort to make it into one big, safe play-area. (This is obviously why travel books are so popular; the general public marvels at those who dare to go to places without sign-posts.) The un-brave new world is at hand. Britain's famous pioneering spirit is being successfully throttled by 'officers' in county towns who don't have anything else to do but create new jobs for new 'officers' who settle on areas like locusts and tidy the place up. They came to ours last year and erected half a dozen signs; three of which pointed to bridleways and footpaths which had changed course one hundred years before and which now point foreigners up a dead-end, into a rubbish-heap and across Giles and Mary Woods' cottage garden. The locals know exactly where their rights of way are anyway. It is passed-on knowledge.

Nothing, least of all common sense, will stop the signing of Britain. We are outnumbered by interferers who want to tell us how to 'go for a walk'. 'Way-marking' and 'trail-marking' are now becoming so universal that they are destroying the very thing they purport to do, namely to show people how beautiful our countryside is. We are also being told, in no uncertain terms, how 'style signing' (as it is called by traffic-management departments) is designed for 'the touring motorist who will be able to spot the easily identifiable series of signs which will direct him to individual attractions . . . The brown signs with white legends and symbols, although distinctive, are considered to be less visually intrusive than other forms of signing as they fit in more harmoniously with the countryside.' What's left of the countryside.

The other day, in a rural backwater of north Norfolk, which, apart from wooden fingerposts and village signs, had suffered little labelling, I found myself on a minor road only to be confronted by a sign telling me I was on a 'Tudor Trail'. Were the trees on either side of me Tudor or had they long been felled to make visible the half-timbered house I expected to see around every corner? I passed some council houses and then I rang up the Norwich Tourist Office. 'It's a ride you take by car, your car. It's a circular route.' 'Why is it called the "Tudor Trail"?' I enquired. 'Well, it passes Blickling Hall which is Tudor.' On its route through Aylesham, Reepham and Holt (almost completely destroyed by fire in 1706, and as un-Tudor a town as you could find), the 'trail' also passes through many modern, Edwardian, Victorian, Regency, Georgian, Queen Anne, Carolean, William and Mary houses and cottages. But none has the same alliterative ring.

As long as twenty-five years ago, a woman wrote to my husband complaining about the mud on a track which went through our field. For me that letter marked the birth of the Wettie Brigade. Did she expect us to tarmac the track? My husband wrote back and told her to buy some gumboots. 'Cycleways' were initiated by 'Beautiful Britain' in 1983. Since then the Wettie Brigade has been infiltrating country life. Its members are writing leaflets as I write, calling themselves 'officers' and designating every nook and cranny as a signable tourist commodity. The Ridgeway, Europe's oldest road, a nice, wide track along the top of a great chalk ridge of downs through Wiltshire and Berkshire, is now signposted from the adjacent motorway. There are no toll booths, gift shops or other tourist purse-emptiers anywhere near the Ridgeway, so why have they done it? Those who want to find the Ridgeway have done so with no difficulty for the last 5,000 years. Why do they suddenly need nannies to tell them where it is? On your 'cycleway', Wetties!

*Candida Lycett Green*

## Dissing

It was a pleasant evening for a party. Although it was September the night was warm enough to keep the balcony doors open, so people who wanted to get away from the hubbub of music and talk could sit and look out across Hampstead Heath. Inside, the guests, ranging in age from ten to seventy-something, all friends of the woman journalist whose birthday we were celebrating, drank, danced, talked, smoked or flirted according to their taste. It was a happy, relaxed event.

The gang must have heard the music and the chatter drifting across the Heath through the open balcony doors. It was easy for them to get in: because of the amount of guests coming and going, neither the street-level door nor the door of the flat, on the fifth floor of the mansion block, were locked. As there were a number of teenagers at the party already, the appearance of several more, all dressed in the uniform of baseball jackets, baggy pants and huge trainers, did not immediately arouse suspicion.

But, quickly, a sense of unease spread. People were looking at these eight young strangers, white and black, male and female, who had moved out through the gathering in ones and twos and now stood around grinning strangely and whispering to each other as they stared at the guests. There had been some pushing, someone's drink had been spilled, voices were raised. Something was Wrong. The music stopped, the lights were turned up in the dancing room. The chatter went on in the other rooms as before, then faces started to appear in the doorway, peering to see our hostess, a beautiful woman in her early thirties in a little black dress, explaining to a pale youth with red-rimmed eyes and an angry stare that she was terribly sorry, but the party was for invited friends only and, as he could see, rather crowded, so, please, could they go now.

The youth swore and his friends laughed. 'We've only just come,' he said, 'you should show some respect.'

'Well,' she said, 'it wasn't very nice of you just to walk in here uninvited, we don't even know you.'

'Now's your chance to get to know us,' said the youth, pulling the ring from a can of beer. 'We ain't done nothing. Yet.' And they all laughed again. Now Rupert came to the fore, something in the City, authoritative:

'Now, look here, it's the girl's party, you're not invited so just get the hell out.' That doesn't go down well. The pale youth swore again, muttering 'Respect' and jerking his arms, as if in some martial arts ritual. Next time he almost shouted it out: 'Respect!'

It was ridiculous, there were eight teenagers in the flat, two of them girls, and they had taken over. Surely one hundred people could rid themselves of eight gate-crashers. Not without a nasty fight, said a small voice in my head. What's he taken? What if he's got a knife? Then something strange happened. A young, trendily dressed guest, who happened to be black and whose name later turned out to be Nigel, sidled up to the gang leader's lieutenant, who was also black, and whispered something persuasively in his ear. The youth nodded at him, reached out to the aggressive one and whispered to him. The leader glared around the room, stretched his hands out in front of him, palms down, and spread them out to either side. 'Not-Enough-Respect!' he yelled, then quickly strode from the room, from the flat, from our sighs of relief, from our lives, followed by all his friends. There were some shouts and bangs from the stairwell, then silence.

They were gone, they didn't come back, and eventually the party picked up steam again. I asked Nigel what he'd said. 'Oh, nothing, really. Just that they weren't invited and that the party wasn't going to continue as long as they were there, but no one wanted any trouble, so, without any disrespect, there wasn't much point in them staying. And I thought it was better to say this quietly, to the less aggressive one, rather than try and confront the nutter.'

That was a while ago. At the time I was puzzled by the way the gatecrasher used the word 'respect'. Now I hear it all the time. Certain sportsmen, especially boxers, use it a lot. So do pop stars and all sorts of people who wear baseball caps backwards. Outside the ring, on the street, in the pub, you got to give 'respect'.

A victim of a knife-wielding mugger in London's King Cross area got a refund, he told the *Guardian* last month, when he returned to the scene of the crime with a large friend and sought out his attacker. The mugger, a crack-dealer, returned the stolen cash and apologised for 'dissing' ('disrespecting') his victim. Respect, it seems, is easily won if you go about your business accompanied by a large friend.

*Tim Minogue*

**Modern tongue**

## Railway rants, No 1

- 'Your on-train team'
- 'We would like to advise customers'
- 'On behalf of myself'
- 'The next station stop will be Carlisle'

# Distant Healing

Earlier this year a group of medical researchers found that being prayed for was good for the health. On the other hand, the scientist Francis Galton found in 1895 that the royals lived no longer than any other prosperous family and enjoyed no better health, although half the population prayed for them each Sunday. That's the good thing about religion and medicine – you can use one or both to prove just about anything.

Ever since Jesus and the laying-on of hands, people have wanted to be healers. It brings a certain status. European royalty picked up the idea. Scrofula, a tuberculous condition of the lymph glands, became known as the King's Evil, treatable by the royal touch. Charles II went in for it in a big way, and even Martin Luther took credit for several miracle cures. By the 1850s, Lourdes had been established as a healing centre, and for the rest of the century there were outbreaks of spiritual healing all over London. Distant Healing takes this concept one stage further – there is no laying on of hands; in fact you never meet your healer. The healer stays put – usually on the other side of the world – and sends out 'healing waves' in your direction. Then, as now, there were all shades of healers, from nice guys to mountebanks.

Searching the Internet for distant healing in the UK, I counted thirty-three 'hits', four times as many as I found when I tried to buy a barbecue online. Most of the healing sites are bound up with ads for astrology magazines, homeopathy, weird crystals and UFOs, so it's anyone's guess where a potty idea ends and delusion begins. Anton of 'Lucence' (formerly of http://members.tripod.co.uk/lucent/ but currently of no fixed address), real name Anton Blackburn, has a slogan: 'Paradise is Now, Lucence is the Way, Anton is your Guide.' He says that the psychically sensitive may even perceive Lucent healing around the limbs of the person needing help. He can be emailed, so I did, with: 'Can you cure lymphoma?' He replied, cryptically: 'The healing power of Lucence is great indeed and of much comfort to many people. I would not claim that I personally can cure anything – I am just the channel for the healing powers, which may or may not work according to our desires.' So if it doesn't work, it's your fault, chummy. On the other hand, if you want 'no hoaxes, no gimmickry, just honest straightforward mediumship', then Laurence Harry says he is your man. He heals pets, too.

I had a week of being distant-healed and stayed the same, apart from a mild bout of food poisoning that followed a dietary indiscretion. Phineas T. Barnum said there's one born every minute, and two to take their money. An outfit called Psychognosis asks punters to send a brief description of their symptoms with a cheque for £620 to an address in Carmarthen.

The redoubtable Edvard Ernst, Professor of Complementary Medicine at Exeter University, has recently performed a clinical trial of distant healing: eighty-four sufferers from warts were randomly assigned to have, or not have, distant healing from any of ten experienced healers. At the end of six weeks they were assessed for number and size of warts, which did not change in either the healed or the control groups. Neither the patients nor the evaluator knew who was being healed and who wasn't, but six people in the healing group and eight in the control group felt subjectively improved. And I daresay the healers felt better, too.

*Caroline Richmond*

# Dogging

Back in the seventies, the word 'dogging' described how Peeping Toms would sneak up on couples who were having sex in cars, and watch them undetected. The etymology of the word is supposedly derived from the voyeur's excuse to his wife: 'I'm just taking the dog for a walk, dear.'

Dogging has evolved. The ease of communication through the Internet has allowed a fundamental change to take place: the voyeurism is consensual. Exhibitionist couples can now invite complete strangers to meet them in secluded outdoor areas, whereupon they can watch them get down to business, and even join in if the couples let them.

It may sound like an obscure activity carried out by a bizarre fringe – but the evidence suggests otherwise. One dogging group has 25,000 members. In a recent survey of Britain's 260 country parks by an academic from Harper Adams College in Newport, two thirds of wardens said that public exhibitionism was their primary problem, ahead of graffiti and poaching.

If it all sounds a little too licentious, we must remember that doggers have a code by which they operate. The 'Ten Dogging Commandments' exist to minimise the obvious risks that come from having sex with complete strangers in a public place, but they also preserve decorum. The third commandment, 'Thou shalt not block thine neighbour's view'", adds: 'Take care thou dost not obscure the sight of thy fellow dogger, and yield the right of way to them who arrived before you.' All sense of propriety is clearly not lost.

By its nature, dogging is a cloak-and-daggers occupation, but the village of Rivington (near Chorley, Lancashire) inadvertently hosted this year's Ultimate Dogging Championships. Apparently, the categories included 'Most Extreme Slapper', which may not be an award to tell the grandchildren about, but it's pleasing to see the Great British Spirit of Competitiveness in such an unlikely context.

The principal dilemma faced by doggers is time-honoured among epicureans: is it legal? Well, if you head to a dogging spot, those present will say it's a legal 'grey area', while a policeman will probably say you're under arrest. There are laws against public sex, and they are concerned with protecting 'unwilling witnesses' from seeing acts of lewdness. But of course the point of dogging is that the witnesses are very willing indeed. Which means its legal status is not unfamiliar either. It's probably illegal, if you get caught.

And dogging's increasing renown is a direct result of celebrities getting caught. Recently the red tops carried a series of stories about the *Eastenders* actor Steve McFadden, who was allegedly dogging around Europe.

If you're a celebrity who is going to have sex in public, a disguise is a good idea, and McFadden apparently chose some items from his pantomime part as Captain Hook. We were not told if any innocent bystanders came across a cockney pirate making love in a continental lay-by, but it is rather hard to know how they would have reacted. The tabloid press vilified McFadden, because his ex-girlfriend alleged that he had forced her to take part in his exploits; yet one senses that the reaction would have been the same had his actions been consensual.

And therein lies the rub. Dogging is clearly absurd, but should those who practise it be maligned? It is a dangerous pastime (for doggers), but it is unlikely to ruin an oldie's day unless he stumbles upon it while with his family, and could even prove educational if he's on his own. What should we make of dogging? Like most sexual crazes, not a lot. Today's youth simply requires an audience for most things it does; if this extends to its bedtime exploits, we shouldn't be surprised.

*Alan White*

# Dress-down Friday

Big business never tires of trying to find novel ways to jolly up its employees. A week barely goes by without the poor hapless cogs in the multinational wheels being shipped off on corporate bonding weekends, frogmarched in to see the corporate shiatsu masseur, or having their offices Feng Shui'd so that the negative energy of the photocopier doesn't get tangled up with the aura of the water cooler.

Concerned, no doubt, that all this faffing around was leaving very little time for anybody actually to do any work, the great Think Tank of Daft Business Concepts dreamt up Dress-down Friday. Every Friday, employees were allowed to leave their formal business attire in the wardrobe and come in to work in their 'own' clothes. Not only did this new morale-boosting initiative keep the workers in the office, but it was also thought to benefit productivity – the workplace would be a friendlier, happier place every Friday as, smiling and comfortable, people would go about their tasks in a haze of soft-focus good will, like the models on the front of knitting patterns.

The idea came from the new technology businesses – software companies and the like – which had sprung up throughout the eighties and nineties and were unfettered by traditional workplace dress codes. But, guess what, when translated to the wider business community of financial institutions, legal firms and multinationals, it didn't really work.

The first sign of problems came when employees were found sometimes to be dressing down rather too much – coming into work looking as if they'd just got out of bed. Corporations responded with guidelines for 'acceptable' casual clothing (polo shirts, blazers, T-shirts) and 'unacceptable' casual clothing ('wrinkled, stained or dirty clothing, beachwear, sportswear – if in doubt, discuss your outfit with your supervisor before wearing it to work').

In fact, workers found 'casual' dress-down Fridays rather fraught: in a suit, one is anonymous, but in one's personal wardrobe, one is suddenly sending out a great many signals about oneself. And in business, only the most positive signals will do. One US law firm, Cadwalader, Wickersham & Taft, even hired *Esquire* magazine and Ralph Lauren to come in and give a seminar on acceptable apparel. Attendance was obligatory.

Books were written – such as Sherry Maysonave's *Casual Power: How to Power Up Your Nonverbal Communication and Dress Down for Success*, which details how to go about giving the best business impression while 'dressed down', how to avoid 'casual confusion syndrome', and how 'certainty leads to casual empowerment'. In fact, far from being freed from sartorial constraints for one day a week, employees were entering a whole new complex (and expensive) semiotic minefield. Moreover, once they had all read the same books on 'dressing down for success' they found themselves dressing the same – for men in particular, a Blairish get-up of chinos and button-down blue denim shirt became de rigueur if one was to avoid the harsh sartorial judgments of others. So much for tossing aside the constraints of a 'uniform'.

So, gradually, people have stopped dressing down and returned to the anonymity of their business suits. One lawyer I spoke to said that he had taken to keeping a jacket and tie at work, in case he had a meeting on a dress-down day with a client who might be less comfortable with his company's more relaxed approach. It meant that he had to make sure that his casual clothes would co-ordinate with his dress-down clothes. In the end he decided it was all just too much trouble. 'There's nothing casual about having to charge off to the loos three times a day to change,' he said.

*Nick Parker*

## Dumbing Down

I am writing this with a smile! In my voice! I have modern hair, as I am writing this, and I am not going to use any long words. Sesquipedalianism – no way! And guess what: I am wearing a woolly jersey! See? I am ordinary! I am as ordinary as you! Maybe even more ordinary . . . but just because I am more ordinary than you doesn't make me special.

Dumbing down, you see – you do see, don't you? and do stop me if it all gets a bit hard – is where it's at. We can get alongside that one, right? We know where it's coming from? Right. Where it's coming from is a sneering hell, boiled from a vile decoction of snobbery, relativism and raw glossy greed by sharp-suited phoneys; what it is, is the latest in the immemorial line of restrictive and joyless orthodoxies masquerading, as always, as a public benefaction. Its spawning-grounds are politics and the media: the two groups which have most to gain from the peddling of infantilising anodynes to a population which otherwise, God help us, might rise up, smash its televisions, burn down Parliament and wipe its collective arse on the newspapers.

Dumbing down isn't just a con, isn't just an insult; it is, at root, cruel and destructive. At its heart lies an abject failure of morality. Imagine if our great public reformers had discovered dumbing down. Walking through the stinking streets, strewn with rot and ordure, they would not have been driven to build sewers, to pipe fresh water and clear the slums; instead, they would have cried 'Mmmm! What a lovely smell! That's how we like to live, too! Aren't you lucky!' And next time you hear some bubble-headed 'personality' put on the radio to introduce great music of which he or she knows nothing; next time you watch some fatuous idiot of an unfunny comedian inexplicably presenting a television programme trivialising important matters, or read a newspaper article mocking and snarling at something fine from a position of invincible ignorance, know that behind them lies some cynical, sneering 'executive' crying 'Mmmm! What a lovely smell!'

Because the worst thing about dumbing down is that it is hypocritical. The people responsible for it are educated, calculating men of well-developed sensibilities who have no share in the restricted, snarling, sound-bitten world-view they peddle. Some, like John Birt, frozen in a sort of inhuman managerial lunacy, may have little apparent understanding of what it is they are doing; but most are all too aware, yet count the rewards worth the shame, and are soon so well-rewarded that they lose the capacity for shame in a welter of self-regard.

And so the process continues. As the old gag has it, 'Eat shit; a hundred billion flies can't be wrong.' The peddlers of dumbing down spot a gap in the market, and so sell shit, telling each other that it's what the public want, it's what they like, it's what they understand, it's all they understand. What cannot be reduced to a slogan or have its sting drawn by a mealy-mouthed 'presenter' must be sneered at and dismissed as 'snobbery'. Great music, art and drama are to be condensed and detoxified; tragedy turned into sentiment; history dismissed as irrelevance; religion relieved of the numinous; and politics stripped of statesmanship and transformed into a branch of public relations.

The dumbers down argue that they are exponents of democracy, but they are either lying or deluded. Democracy turns upon the principle of an informed electorate, not upon its stupefaction. There is nothing democratic about a party political system which battles solely for the control and manipulation of the public's prejudices. The commanders of the Roman Empire knew that after they had won the battle, they had to win hearts and minds; now our politicians seek to win the reptilian hindbrain, as though the exercise of our franchise were co-located with the part that controls our genitals.

Strange and disagreeable as it may be, the slightly improving odour which emanated from H. G. Wells and Bernard Shaw and the Mechanics Institutes was far less redolent of patronising infantilisation than the sweeter, fruitier, vanilla-and-peachier hogo which shimmers off Disney and Blair, the civety cat-reek of Mandelson, the watermelon insubstantiality of Hague and the honking, faecal, butyric stench of the Murdoch bloids and their imitators. Those are the real odours of inequality, keeping the proles ticking over in their telly-struck, drum-deadened, dogmeat-pie oubliettes. The do-gooding improvers of a century ago might have been a bit sandals-and-fruit-juice, the tiniest touch oopsie-la, but at least they had more hope than cynicism, did not confuse statistics with judgement, believed perhaps not only that people deserved better, but that there was a better for them to deserve. Now, in the hunt for power and profit and in the name of relativism and market research, instead of being enticed and encouraged, we are indulged, offered spurious and impertinent approval ('Yes! We all like football and fish fingers too!') and treated like children, overwhelmed with slogans, sound-bites, confessional television, proliferating admonitions, vacuous grinning young women, jerks in jerseys, photo-opportunities.

But that's where the money is, so . . . hey, I'm not one of your snobs. Not me. Rameau, Suetonius, Primo Levi, Shelley, J. S. Mill? Never heard of them! Give me football any day! Look! Still wearing my jersey! Football! Oasis!

Still smiling! Modern hair! Hello? Mr Murdoch? I didn't mean it! It was a joke! I'm available . . .

*Michael Bywater*

*'Eye of newt, wing of bat, twizzler of turkey.'*

# Echelon

Echelon is an intelligence-gathering operation set up during the Cold War, and is now funded and operated by the intelligence agencies of five nations: the United States, the United Kingdom, Canada, Australia and New Zealand, operating out of, among other places, Menwith Hill in North Yorkshire and GCHQ in Cheltenham.

The growth of the digital age has given it an unprecedented ability to snoop on just about anything. The system can apparently process over three billion communications every day, including telephone calls, emails, satellite transmissions, Internet downloads, faxes and so on. Using powerful software to filter the data and 'sniff' out certain types of communication, Echelon can search for certain keywords, or topics. This work is said to be aided by some 55,000 agents who are involved in anything from searching through data manually to planting bugging devices on deep-sea transmission cables. It is also rumoured that Echelon has even more invasive capabilities, such as being able to use your mobile phone as a tracking device, and also to remotely disable its ring tone and use it to eavesdrop on your conversations. If you send an email to a friend commenting on the lousiness of last night's episode of *Big Brother*, or even remark on this at the bus stop while carrying your mobile phone in your pocket, it is possible that Echelon will have heard you.

Now it would not be unusual to find this kind of talk on some paranoid conspiracy theory website, but concrete evidence of the existence of Echelon has come from a report released recently by the European Parliament – a body not generally known for its over-excitability. The report (entitled *Document in Preparation for a Report on the Existence of a Global system for Intercepting Private and Commercial Communications*) presents strong evidence not only that the network exists, but that it routinely listens in on domestic companies and private individuals. Other sources claim that it has also been used for industrial espionage. It has been said that the French lost a $6 billion contract for Airbus with the Saudi government to Boeing and McDonnell Douglas thanks to Echelon's intercepting of faxes and telephone calls.

However, all that is clearly a side issue. What you all obviously want to know is: are the people at Echelon reading our emails and laughing at them? Have they intercepted those photographs we have just emailed to the grandchildren in Australia, printed them out and stuck them on their staff noticeboard for all to snigger at? Alarmingly, the European Parliament's report admits that snooping into civilian emails may well be going on, and advises us all to encrypt them. There are a number of ways to do this, such as using specially designed software programmes like PGP, which stands for Pretty Good Privacy (although given the information regarding Echelon's efficacy, I hope that the manufacturers will soon be upgrading to Bloody Marvellous Privacy), or the splendidly titled 'Hushman'. Both of these work like a virtual Enigma machine, scrambling your emails as you send them, and only allowing users who have 'keys' assigned by yourself to unscramble them.

Still, if you're really concerned about your electronic communications being bugged, sniffed, filtered, tracked or scanned, why not embrace a technology which is impervious to all digital snooping, and write a letter?

*Nick Parker*

**Modern tongue**

## Railway rants, No 2

'There are delays on the Central line, the Circle line and the Hammersmith and City line. The Bakerloo line southbound is suspended. King's Cross station is closed due to a security alert. The Jubilee line is experiencing signalling problems in the Neasden area. There is a good service running on all other lines.' (Which other lines are left?)

## Empathy

Do you think that children learning to read should be taught the sound of individual letters? That children learning to add should not be allowed to use a calculator? That children learning history should be taught facts? That children should be taught in rows, and not be left to wander around, learning from 'experience'? If you believe any of these things, watch out. You might be labelled a 'traditionalist', the very worst form of abuse that the Education Establishment can hurl at you.

These 'traditional' beliefs have been exiled from Britain's schools for a generation, expelled by the fanatical egalitarianism of 'progressive' theorists who have managed to ruin the education of thousands of children. Their greatest coup was the slow subversion of the National Curriculum and the examination system; and nowhere have they left a clearer mark than on the history syllabus.

The Party slogan in Orwell's 1984 encapsulates why history matters: 'Who controls the past controls the future. Who controls the present controls the past.' Those who control the history syllabus currently taught in many schools do not like Britain, and they want to change it. New Britain requires New History.

Evidence of New History is easy to find. British history – particularly political and military history – no longer forms the cornerstone of what children learn. It has been elbowed out of schools by ersatz themes, such as 'Race

Relations in Multi-Cultural Society since 1945'. Gone is the notion that history should impart the narrative of our past in a methodical manner. Empathy and interpretation of sources, not dates and events, now underpin history teaching in our schools.

The analysis of sources is a sophisticated skill. Students need a mental framework of dates and events so they can put the source in context. To be examined properly, students should be expected to construct an argument, supported by factual knowledge, which explains the source's relevance. The GCSE does not demand this of students. Many questions simply ask for students' views, not their knowledge.

Consider one question on 'Aspects of British Social and Economic History', for those who have studied 'Cinema, Radio and TV since 1945'. Students are given sources including a quote from J. B. Priestley and a cover of the *TV Times*. Of the five questions that follow, three could be answered without any knowledge whatsoever. Pupils are asked, for example, whether they agree that, before 1980, television was 'more of a curse than a blessing to British society'.

These absurd questions are the consequence of children being taught not periods of history, but historical themes, such as 'Poverty 1815–1990'. This is a massive topic, to which scholars have devoted their entire careers. For a proper understanding, teenagers would need to know much more than could ever be expected of them: some basic economic theory, the philosophical theories which underpinned the Victorian approach to poverty, the political landscape, the changing social fabric – the list is long. As they cannot know this aged sixteen, they are asked instead to empathise with those who lived in poverty. The questions are fatuous and leading: 'Why did unemployed people in the 1930s resent the means test?', or 'Why did the poor hate the New Poor Law?'

To answer these questions, children need to empathise with what it was like to be means-tested and poor. This risks a mild, subtle form of indoctrination: the means test was 'bad', the New Poor Law 'bad'. There are no questions like 'Why did the middle-classes like the capitalist system?' Not that there should be: values and 'feelings' should not be allowed to push facts and knowledge out of the window.

'Themes' have conquered the history syllabus and gradually evicted British political history, which has been reduced to claiming squatter's rights in various syllabuses. Many children study history for only a few years, but could waste some of this precious opportunity being taught themes like 'Urbanisation and the Health of the People'. Our nation's past has succumbed to the cultural relativism of the politically correct, by whose diktat it is wrong to teach teenagers British history to the exclusion of other cultures. Yet if history does anything, it should give children an understanding of how the present relates to the past. It should impart knowledge which acts as a grid reference, thereby helping children to understand other cultures. If the current trend continues, children will learn more about the sociological reasons for poverty than the milestones of our island's history.

Why has the teaching of knowledge become so unpopular? Knowledge stands for tradition, experience, heritage, authority. These values fly in the face of child-centred theories, which have indoctrinated countless teachers into believing that children should be free to express themselves; that a child's opinion, however idiotic, is just as valid as anyone else's; and that tradition is something that a child should learn from his or her own 'experience'. Knowledge can also be tested, exposing the harsh reality that some children are better-informed than others – a fact which egalitarians cannot stomach. And learning facts requires effort and discipline: children need to be taught them in a structured manner, requiring a return to whole-class teaching. The teacher cannot be a 'facilitator'.

Worst of all, real history exposes harsh realities that some on the left would prefer to ignore and cannot afford to admit. The world is unfair; humans are unequal. 'History is the handmaiden of authority,' wrote J. H. Plumb. The authority of the history that used to be taught in schools was grounded in the purity of factual knowledge. It is now being abused by educationists who think 'their' history is superior, and who are forcing children to learn about Britain's past from the progressive perspective. L. P. Hartley's description of the past in his novel *The Go-Between* is being realised: it is indeed 'a foreign country'.

*George Bridges*

# eXtreme Sports

Cast aside any images of athletic men and women braving Everest or doing the Cresta Run. This is no Oxford Dangerous Sports Society. Neither athleticism nor courage is required. eXtreme sports include rollerblading, skateboarding, surfing and wakeboarding. The latter is especially daft: instead of being towed on water-skis, you are towed on a windsurfer and jump over the wake of the boat.

None of this would matter if it weren't for the arrival of the eXtreme Sports Channel. EX TV is desperately trying to legitimise the adult men (not teenage boys) who spend their lives mastering silly tricks (sorry, 'stunts') which no circus could charge for. And there are championships. The winning 'athlete' is judged on levels of 'cool' and skill. Very simply, they have taken their playground breaks a little too far. And herein, I hope, lies their nemesis.

My solution? What is needed is a 'rebranding exercise'. We rebrand eXtreme sports as 'PLaYGRouND' (like what I've done with the vowels? I can just see the T-shirts), and we introduce a whole new raft of traditional events: hopscotch, tag, British Bulldog and kick the can. Old school teams would form themselves into regional leagues. With our own TV channel, we can look forward to a national cup final in all four sports by the time Wembley is rebuilt.

*James Pembroke*

# Flash Mob

One evening in June 2004, dozens of people converged on the concourse of Victoria station. They donned headphones, hit the play buttons on their Walkmans and bopped to music only they could hear. Bemused commuters looked on as these dancers, who were dotted all over the station, boogied away in disco solos. 'Mobile clubbing' is just the latest guise of the flash mob phenomenon – a craze for random acts of pointlessness, which has appeared around the world in the last eighteen months.

Flash mobbing, also known as 'flocking' and 'Movimiento Instantáneo', was pioneered in New York in 2003. The point of this self-confessedly pointless movement is the apparently random convergence of strangers in a public location. Flash mob organisers, who generally work anonymously or under pseudonyms, issue instructions through text messages and emails.

The person credited as the architect of flash mobbing is the American technology writer Howard Rheingold. He has since published a book, *Smart Mobs: The Next Social Revolution*, which explores the way in which new technologies can enable and inspire collective action. There are certainly examples of where technology has been used for serious social purposes. In the Philippines, political activists ousted President Estrada by arranging demonstrations through mass text messaging, and in the UK, the Stop the War coalition has used its website to mobilise thousands of anti-war marchers.

Most flash mob events, however, seem less concerned with social change than with anarchic, surreal merry-making. Flash mobbing has no ideological agenda. The aim is purely one of entertainment – to bring a few moments of joy or surprise to weary commuters and harassed shoppers. In New York, a hundred people turned up at Macy's department store in the home furnishing section. The assembled mobbers told the bewildered staff that they were looking for a 'love rug' on which to host orgies in their suburban commune. In Central Park, mobbers tweeted like birds and crowed like roosters. Over in San Francisco, hundreds of people span around in circles, like children. In Berlin, a mass of people wearing silly hats congregated outside the US embassy on Unter den Linden, popped champagne bottles and drank repeated toasts 'to Natasha'. And in Dortmund, a group assembled in a department store where the assembled mobbers each ate a banana.

Initially, the Brits were slow to take on the flash mobbing phenomenon. Eventually, though, they overcame their reticence and the first British flash mob event took place in August 2003. The proprietor of Sofas UK in Soho was baffled when, at 6.30 pm one evening, a friendly crowd of 300 people suddenly descended on his store. Their intention was, apparently, to look at sofas. With the timing of a Greek chorus, they suddenly exclaimed in unison, 'Oh, wow! What a sofa!', burst into applause and left, as quickly as they had arrived.

Who are these flash mobbers? They are not, as you might expect, a collective of unemployed actors and performance artists, desperate for some attention. In fact, it would seem that most mobbers are white twenty- and thirty-somethings, often working in professions such as IT. This makes a lot of sense. After all, IT workers are techno-savvy, with access to the communication networks that enable flash mobs to co-ordinate.

In a society that is struggling with its loss of community and its increasingly isolated lifestyles, the notion of joining a group to indulge in random acts of harmless fun is a refreshingly social one. Perhaps the flash mobbers are consciously making a stand against today's individualism and materialism.

At the same time, it seems just a little disappointing that the energy and organisation that brings about a flash mob is not employed to more world-changing ends. Would it not be more fulfilling to gather together to fight for human rights or to protest against the destruction of the natural environment?

*Emma Harding*

# Focus Group

'England has done one thing: it has invented and established public opinion which is an attempt to organise the ignorance of the community and to elevate it to the dignity of physical force,' Oscar Wilde wrote of late Victorian Britain. His words seem even more appropriate to our own age, where the views of the public on every possible subject are now treated with grotesque reverence. So, attempting to match the ever-shifting moods of public opinion, the Established Church feels compelled to abandon its traditions. The monarchy watches the vast, lachrymose crowds outside Buckingham Palace and promises to change, while successive leaders of the Conservative Party don baseball caps and declare that they are 'caring'.

In this constant drive to be 'in tune' with the public, institutions, political parties and businesses increasingly rely on market research to tell them what 'ordinary people' are thinking. It is not surprising, therefore, that market research has become one of the great growth industries of the last decade. 'Real growth has continued at levels of around 10 per cent for some years now,' says the Association of Market Survey Organisations. It is estimated that the total size of the industry – led by companies such as National Opinion Polls and Taylor Nelson AGB – could be more than £750 million.

Market research can be divided into two types of methodology. First, there is the 'quantitative research' which relies on asking a large, representative sample of the public its opinion on a certain product or issue. It is from such research that we get all those statistics which so intrigue the media, such as '41 per cent of couples have had sex in the kitchen' or '88 per cent of the public don't believe the war in Iraq is perceived as effective'. The problem with such numbers, say market researchers, is that they provide only a superficial picture of public attitudes. And they do not explain why such opinions are held.

It was to answer such questions that the second, 'qualitative' method of polling has been developed. Qualitative researchers gather together small 'focus groups' of about ten people and get them into a discussion about, say, BBC programming or a new make of car. Each group can be drawn from a different sector of the population. One group might therefore comprise only women under thirty; another might be made up of affluent professionals. The discussion is led by a moderator from the research company and the views of the participants are recorded, analysed and then submitted in a report to the client. The appeal of this method is that it provides a deeper understanding of public attitudes beyond bald statistics. Mike Imms, a leading practitioner in the field, explains: 'Qualitative research developed in Britain in the sixties because marketing organisations found that conventional polling methods were giving them inadequate answers.' About 13 per cent of market research is now carried out in this way.

There are a number of methodological drawbacks to focus groups. Because the samples are so small, they can never be representative. Groups can be dominated by a few confident individuals. Some participants may be fearful of expressing their views, especially politically incorrect ones on subjects such as homosexuality or race. Nor does extensive market research always guarantee success in the commercial world. Before the launch of its 'New Coke', Coca-Cola tested the brand on 190,000 people. It flopped dismally. The corporate rebranding of British Airways, including the replacement of the Union flag with ethnic graffiti on its planes, involved an expensive programme of polls and focus groups, yet proved so unpopular with staff and the public that BA eventually changed their planes back to how they'd been before.

The BBC's reliance on focus groups has been bitterly attacked by programme makers, who complain that their findings now carry more weight than the instincts of drama bosses. Michael Wearing, the man responsible for major successes such as *Boys from the Black Stuff* and *Pride and Prejudice* resigned as head of drama, after his proposed new serial was shelved because focus-group research suggested that viewers might find the plot boring. On this basis, TV producer Kenith Trodd pointed out, *The Singing Detective*, a story about a man with a hideous skin condition lying in hospital, would probably never have been made.

Allowing focus groups to determine our television watching may be bad enough, but even worse is the way market research now drives the thinking of our political parties, especially Labour. It was under Neil Kinnock in the 1980s that Labour first began to use focus groups to influence policy, but now, under Blair, they have become all-powerful. In fact, the focus group has been institutionalised as one of the estates of the realm. Shortly after gaining power in 1997, ministers announced the creation of a 5,000-strong 'People's Panel' to test public reaction to new and existing policies. Costing tens of thousands of pounds, the initiative includes telephone surveys, 'citizens' juries' and smaller focus groups made up of the correct gender and ethnic mix. Amidst this frenzy of political marketing, the question arises: why should public policy be dictated by those selected at random rather than those chosen democratically by the electorate?

Focus groups might be fine for testing a new brand of lager but they are no substitute for government.

*Leo McKinstry*

# Further Information

Whenever I put my card into my HSBC cash machine, the screen lights up and says: 'Please wait a moment – we are dealing with your request,' and I tell it, 'No, you are not! I have not made a request yet! I have only put my card in!' but it never listens to me, and that's because it's all part of the upgrading of everything. Everything is being made to sound better than it is, or than it was. That's why the man on the train, after you have been stationary for a quarter of an hour, says he is sorry for the delay and that he has no idea yet why it has happened, 'but as soon as we have further information, we will let you know'. Further information? They haven't got any information! How can they give us further information?

Everything is upgraded. The man on the train saying those things used to be a ticket collector, but now he is a train manager, or steward, or something. There used to be a Complaints department, but now it is Customer Services, thus switching the focus from the *bad* thing you are complaining about to the *good* things they will do about it. There used to be people in the office. Now there is a 'team'. They used to be 'personnel', but now they are 'Human Resources'.

A woman on the phone recently asked me to confirm my address. I waited to hear what she thought it was, so I could confirm it. She didn't know what it was. What she meant was 'Can you *tell* me your address?' It's all of a piece with the way we now say that we 'target' something, instead of just aiming at it, so that we can 'impact' it, instead of just affecting it. It's upgrading. Even 'information' has been upgraded to 'intelligence'. 'We raided the house acting on intelligence', say the police. No, you didn't. Intelligence didn't come into it. Just faulty facts.

That's it. Oh, no, it isn't. My wife wishes to add something. She says her most hated phrase is 'their loved ones'. She wants to know why 'their relatives' has to be upgraded to 'their loved ones'.

That's it now.

*Miles Kington*

# Gateway Opportunity

I hate the word 'gateway', which has become popular in marketing. Estate agents describing a 'gateway opportunity' for example. That'll be a shop next to a road. And I particularly don't like it when an unremarkable town describes itself as a 'gateway' to some local, or not so local, attraction. Wooler in Northumberland is marketed as 'the gateway to the Cheviots'. It should more properly be called 'the arsehole of the Cheviots'. I'm sure that would attract more tourists.

And I don't like it when a business becomes a 'one-stop shop'. A blacksmith used to be the place to go for horse shoes, buckets, plough repairs, all sorts of things. But smithies didn't feel the need to describe their shed as a 'one-stop shop'. They're only saying it because it rhymes, not because it means anything worth saying.

And I don't like people who describe themselves as 'facilitators'. All that means is that they provide a facility, i.e. they do something. Everyone with a bloody job does something. The twats. The fact that you do something is not relevant to what you actually do.

*Chris Donald*

# Gob Ons

A Gob On is any period detail on a house which obstinately refuses to belong to the era of the building to which it is attached. You know the sort of thing – Doric columns, decorative Tudorbethan timber, Georgian panelled doors on garages, carriage lights, fake leaded windows, wraparound porches and Rococo balustrades. An excellent specimen would be a 1930s semi surrounded by gold-tipped iron railings, set off by regal stone lions clutching shields between their paws. Think Gothic-style windows 'leaded' in bright brass-coloured plastic.

We British are particularly prone to this kind of ersatz nonsense. A building company called Walker Residential even builds the Gob On tendency into the very heart of its developments. One such is Deanery Grange, which they describe as giving 'the impression of a house which has evolved over time, with its decorative oak timber, painted render, tile hanging and oriel window harking back to seventeenth-century origins. As time passed one can imagine a fine Georgian-style wing being added featuring a stone-pillared portico with balcony above.'

Perhaps it's our obsession with period dramas that has us reaching for the carriage lights in B&Q? Perhaps we were all so traumatised by the hideous modernist excesses of the sixties that we've retreated into a sort of architectural infantilism? All I know is that if I see a house with fake Roman columns bestriding a uPVC front door, it does actually make me want to gob on it.

*Emma Harding*

# Grunge*

'Grunge' is perhaps the most accurately descriptive label for any genre of pop music since 'punk'. Grunge is exceptionally loud, simplistic, dirty guitar music. Like all previous musical cults, it is designed primarily to annoy parents. It is about growing your hair, wearing appalling clothes and smelling horrible. It is about believing that your emotional teenage turmoil is best expressed by instruments played badly accompanied by lots of earnest shouting (which to be fair, it probably is.) It is the late sixties and early seventies reborn. It is, in short, a wee bit familiar.

Still, it must be remembered that it's tough being a teenager these days. Once upon a time teenagers had Real Parents, who wore cardigans, thought that Cliff Richard was a danger to society and that a 'festival' involved taking a basket of vegetables to church in September. These days, parents themselves go on endlessly about how they saw Hendrix on the Isle of Wight, and drone on about how Glastonbury isn't what it used to be now you can't climb over the fence and get in for free.

---

* Yes, we do realise that grunge music is now utterly dead and gone. Over. Kaput. No matter – we're sure another re-hashing of the sixties and seventies is just around the corner. The name may be different but the formula will be the same. Perhaps you'd like to scribble out 'grunge' and add in the name of the new trend for yourself. There's interactivity for you. Who said books were dead, eh?

But teenagers are resourceful creatures, and perhaps Grunge is the best revenge of all: what could be more irksome to their parents than serving up their parents' own youth to them, reheated and recycled. Just to remind them how embarrassing all that long hair and smelly clothing was. And what's more, teenagers act as though they thought it up all by themselves. Stealing their parents' past is clever enough. Failing even to acknowledge the theft is positively ingenious.

*Marcus Berkmann*

**Modern tongue**

## Railway rants, No 3

- 'Warning: professional pickpockets operate in this area.'
- Thank you for choosing to travel with South-Eastern Rail.'

  (Except that South-Eastern Rail holds a monopoly over the route and therefore no choice was ever actually possible . . .)

# Hello Kitty

Hello Kitty is a small white cat with a red ribbon behind her ear. She was born in 1974. Her hobbies include reading, cooking, making friends and being worth over 30 billion dollars a year.

Hello Kitty started life as a cartoon graphic dreamed up by the Japanese company Sanrio in order to sell plastic purses, and has grown into a pink-tinted, fluffy-edged worldwide phenomenon. Her popularity is such that you could slap her blank little visage on to barrels of toxic waste and people would queue round the block to take the stuff off your hands. In Singapore recently, McDonald's decided to give away limited-edition Hello Kitty plastic toys with their kiddies' 'Happy Meals'. On the first day of the offer the country's McDonald's outlets were swamped by over 250,000 people. Thousands of Singaporeans waited throughout the night outside the restaurants, and the national papers regretfully reported that several 'outbreaks of ungraciousness' had occurred, which quickly became known as the Hello Kitty Riots.

Of course, barely a year passes without some new cartoon tat appearing with the intention of separating children from their pocket money, but what has set Hello Kitty apart from other badly drawn cash cows has been the extent to which she has appealed not only to children but to adults as well. This is particularly the case in Japan. While Japanese schoolgirls are holding their socks up with Hello Kitty sock glue – yes, really – fully grown

Japanese businesswomen (Hello Kitty is more popular with women than men, but only just) with proper jobs and clean bills of mental health are toasting their bread in Hello Kitty toasters (it burns Kitty's face on to your bread), driving to work in Hello Kitty cars, paying for their sushi with Hello Kitty credit cards and even using Hello Kitty sanitary towels.

This embracing of a mawkish, saccharine icon by so-called grown-ups the length and breadth of Japan is part of a wider Japanese trend for all things *kawaii* (pronounced to rhyme with Hawaii), which translates as 'cute'. Kawaii is seen as a virtue; to surround oneself with kawaii trinkets is desirable. The sickly-sweet shockwaves of kawaii are being felt everywhere. When Panasonic were launching a new state-of-the-art portable email device with built-in camera, they thought that the most important design consideration would be how many pixels the screen could display. They were wrong. After consulting their focus groups, it turned out that what they should be concentrating their efforts on was making it a cute colour, with a keyboard that did not chip girls' fingernails.

There are a number of reasons for this explosion of suffocating cuteness in the Far East. Partly it is because there is not the same pressure on children to put away their childish things as they make the transition into adulthood; partly it is because in Japan the global obsession with youth is particularly focused on young girls, whose tastes and whims are seen as the very touchstone of coolness; but largely it seems to be that Hello Kitty, her boyfriend Dear Daniel and her myriad of kawaii chums act as an effective emotional pressure valve for the stressful Japanese way of life. The traditional samurai-like values of punishing hard work and self-discipline have clearly taken their toll, and what better way to unwind after a 15-hour day than with a massage from a Hello Kitty shiatsu cushion? 'The lovely Hello Kitty doll helps us relax a little,' says a grown-up Tokyo bank manager, although it is distinctly possible that he and the rest of Japan are suffering from some kind of poisoning from the fumes from all that sock glue.

*Nick Parker*

## Hyper-parenting

A child is born. A time of joy and wonder. But remember that each second is precious to your child's development. You want her to get into a good school – yes? And to excel at her SATS, 11-plus, GCSEs, A/S and A-levels? Of course you'll want her to get into a good university? And to find a well-paid, high-status job that will be the envy of all your friends? These are just some of the pleasures that await the hyper-parent. They are, however, pleasures that must be earned through much parental effort and investment.

The good news is that hyper-parenting can begin even before your baby is born. Play Mozart and whale music to your bump, in order to stimulate mental activity and ensure increased brainpower. When the baby finally emerges, surround her with bright and stimulating toys. She may seem more interested in the buttons on your shirt or a discarded crisp packet, but persevere nonetheless. You might also want to invest in some educational videos, like those produced by the Baby Einstein Company. One such product is a DVD called *The Baby Galileo: Discovering the Sky*, which promises a multisensory learning experience 'investigating the stars, the sun, clouds, planets and whirling galaxies far away' and features a musical score by Mozart, Chopin, Strauss and Tchaikovsky.

Now spend hours reading Ofsted reports and league tables and surfing the Internet in order to work out which primary school is most desirable. Do all you can to secure that all-important catchment area address. Take out a vast mortgage, pretend you live with your mother, or exchange your comfortable three-bed semi with garden for a one-room flat with rising damp.

Once your child has started school, hire tutors in maths, English and verbal reasoning to prepare him or her for secondary school entrance exams. Music lessons might also give your child an advantage. Free time? Of course that's important too. Treat your child to a stimulating tour of your local museums and galleries, making sure to point out any interesting architectural features along the way. Holidays should not be wasted – they provide a wonderful opportunity to slot in some extra maths coaching and tennis lessons. Not to mention the Japanese classes.

Unless you do all this, your child is likely to end up as a member of the teenage hordes we all know about from our newspapers. Overweight, under-motivated and out of control, subject to police curfews and Anti-Social Behaviour Orders. It seems we no longer trust our children to turn out reasonably well-adjusted and intellectually curious. And yet there was a world before Gina Ford's parenting regimes and school league tables. Why have we forgotten?

Parents are full of fear. We don't trust our education system to deliver the learning experience we would wish for our children. We take no comfort in the ever-improving GCSE and A-level results as we worry that they merely demonstrate falling standards. We read countless newspaper reports on childhood obesity, but our terror of paedophiles means we won't let our children run off to the local park to burn off the calories. We also live in an era when it's very difficult for a family to live on just one salary. Both parents feel compelled to work and both feel guilty at the lack of time spent with their children. On top of this, the media besieges them with notions of 'good' and 'bad' parenting, so that 'quality time' has come to mean something commodified and organised.

There is huge pressure on parents to keep their children mentally and physically stimulated at all times.

But children need time and space to develop their independence and exercise their imaginations, to play with friends and siblings, perhaps even to discover the pleasures of reading, writing and drawing for themselves. Good parenting does demand stimulating young minds with new challenges and experiences, but surely the true goal of parenting should be more to do with fostering feelings of happiness and self-worth and less to do with educational success? I'm willing to bet that most of our parents didn't have our weekends scheduled and time-tabled down to the last violin lesson. And look at the illiterate, innumerate, uncultured hoodlums we turned out to be.

*Emma Harding*

# Identity Theft

What is identity theft?

Identity theft is a way of selling paper shredders to people who don't really need them.

I know this because I have seen many advertisements from paper shredder manufacturers informing me that identity theft is Britain's fastest-growing crime. Luckily, before I could sink too far into the gloom such a growing menace presented, the rest of the advertisement informed me that a paper shredder would stop the identity thief in his tracks. Hooray! Another problem solved by the glorious mechanism of free market capitalism.

Identity theft is also a way of selling identity cards to people who don't really need them.

I know this because I have heard many government spokesmen informing me that terrorism is the Briton's greatest threat today. Luckily, before I could sink too far into the gloom such a growing menace presented, the government spokesman informed me that an identity card would stop the terrorist in his tracks. Hooray! Another problem solved by the glorious mechanism of our admirable government.

Identity theft is also an existential concept that has been created in order to lull a disenchanted and often spiritually and philosophically lost populace into thinking that their largely meaningless lives have both significance and worth. I know this because I have thought both long and hard on the concept of 'identity theft' and have come to the conclusion that for the 'theft' of an 'identity' to take place there must be an 'identity' there to begin with. Given that we live in an age when so many of us worry about 'who we really are', the very fact that someone thinks it worthwhile to steal our identity is a glorious vindication of our very existence.

Follow this line of reasoning, and becoming a victim of identity theft is not something to be feared, but something to be embraced as a positive appreciation of our social worth. Indeed, the person to be pitied is not the one whose identity was purloined, but the one whose identity was not deemed worthy of nicking.

On the other hand maybe I'm getting the wrong end of the stick. This has sometimes happened in the past. Maybe the real problem with 'identity theft' is its name. Maybe calling the phenomenon 'identity' theft psychologically shifts the responsibility to the victim of the crime.

But, in truth, when you consider what actually happens, no one ever really steals your identity, they only steal your identification. And it is your identification – e.g. your PIN number – that gives the criminal access to the systems where your money is kept. So maybe what we're really talking about is 'identification theft'. But phrase it like that and doesn't it sound like what's really at fault is a vastly complicated system that isn't secure, as opposed to the problem being your own personal inability to shred your Tesco Club Card statements?

Also 'identification theft' sounds nowhere near as

emotive as 'identity theft'. The first makes it sound like only a thing is being stolen. The second makes it sound like *you* are being stolen. And if you want to motivate people to act, to spend money they don't need to spend, to approve of laws they don't need to approve, it's always better to colour your arguments with emotive fears rather than rational ones.

*Rohan Candappa*

*'It's the worst case of identity theft we've ever seen.'*

# Innit

Yes yes, we're perfectly well aware that if Chaucer popped up today we wouldn't understand a word of what he was saying, and yes of course we know that only the most tedious type of pedantic missed-the-whole-point-about-the-evolution-of-language bore bangs on about how the word 'gay' *really* means 'happy' or a 'kid' is just a young goat, and we've read *Noblesse Oblige* thank you very much so we know that posh people do it just as much as yoofs, and we couldn't agree more with Stephen Fry that it's simply marvellous how 'book' is the new word for 'cool' because typing in 'cool' into a mobile phone predictive text thingy brings up 'book' and of course we concur, this does all point to the rich potency of the English language and there's nothing we'd like less than a hatchet-faced bunch of linguistic fascists getting all worked up like the French with their 'le weekend' hand-wringing *but even so* –

There is something so teeth-grindingly, stomach-churningly fuck-witted about some of today's slang that, try as I might, all my linguistic relativity just turns to ashes and all I'm left with is the distinct impression that YOUNG PEOPLE THESE DAYS SPEAK LIKE MORONS.

Perhaps this is because swearing is no longer taboo, and yoofs have to find another way of making us feel like the barbarians are at the gates. Perhaps it was ever thus. I don't really care. All I know is that they sound mad. Deranged. Like the bit of their brain that controls language has been attacked by some special kind of wasting disease, leaving their thoughts so garbled they couldn't even hold a conversation with George Bush. And the most ear-bendingly gruesome symptom of this terrible disease is one tiny word: Innit.

In order to experience the exquisite pain that this phrase can cause, let's get a little etymological: Innit started life as an abbreviation of 'isn't it?' It was popular with young people trying to sound black. So for instance, the statement 'This is your copy of *The Oldie*, isn't it?' in yoofspeak, would be: 'This is your copy of *The Oldie*, innit?'

Now you may not like the sound of it, but what can you do? 'Isn't it' itself, is, after all, a contraction of 'is not it?'

But then something truly horrendous happened. 'Innit' mutated into a word in its own right. A sort of all-purpose affirmation or exclamation, with utter disregard for grammatical sense. Thus:

'Little Bobby has just got an ASBO, hasn't he?'

'Little Bobby has just got an ASBO, innit?'

and now it ranges across yoofspeak with reckless abandon:

YOOF ONE: 'Yo, look at my new car innit.'

YOOF TWO: 'Innit!'

YOOF ONE: 'What are you looking at innit.' [note that question mark no longer necessary]

If that wasn't enough to get you weeping into your *Fowler's English Usage*, here's a brief tour of some other choice slang words currently tripping off the tongues of the nation's yoof:

'D'you wanna kotch tonight?'

'Nah, allow that, man. I'm gonna get mash up.'

*Translation:*

'Would you like to relax and stay in tonight?'

'No I don't want to do that. I'd rather go out and get inebriated.'

'That girl be butters. She ain't gonna get no tings tonight.'

*Translation:*

'That girl is unattractive. She won't find a man tonight.'

'He's got nuff dirty choons, d'you get me?'

*Translation:*

'He has a large collection of good songs.'

[NB 'D'you get me?' just added in for effect]

'Shut your mouth, you brute. You're caning my earpiece.'

*Translation:*

'Be quiet, you lout. You are hurting my ears with your loud shouting.'

'Laaater! It's pissing down out there.'

*Translation:*

'Oh my goodness! It's raining very heavily outside.'

'Did you clock those hood rats on the corner?'

'Allow them. You're well prang, innit?'

*Translation:*

'Did you see the young thugs on the street corner?'

'Don't worry about them. You are rather paranoid, aren't you?'

'Come you borrow me a nugget.'

*Translation:*

'Please can you lend me a pound?'

'This is dry. Come we duss.'

*Translation:*

'This isn't very good. Let's go.'

'I gotta kotch with the olds tonight.'

'Pshhh, shame! That sounds long.'

*Translation:*

'I have to stay at home with my parents this evening.'

'[Derogatory mocking]! That doesn't sound like very much fun.'

'That's the car I like innit. That car is boom.'

'Seen.'

*Translation:*

'I like that car. That car is very nice.'

'I see.'

'Tonight I'm just gonna kotch at my drum.'
'Seen. Come round my drum if you want.'
'Nah, mate. I'll get jacked round your manor innit.'
*Translation:*
'Tonight I'm going to stay at home.'
'I see. You can come to my house if you like.'
'No way. I will be mugged in your area.'

'That brer's a football bandit.'
'Innit. He's a veteran.'
*Translation:*
'That boy is very good at football.'
'Yes, you're right. He's been playing for a long time.'

No doubt they'll all be out of fashion by the time this book is in print. But that's just the nature of slang, innit.

*Sonali Chapman/Nick Parker*

# Investors in People

Investors in People says it's a national quality standard which sets a level of good practice for improving an organisation's performance through its people. Since it was started in 1991, Sainsbury's, W H Smith, Boots, M&S and 34,000 other companies have been accredited. To become an accredited company you must prove, among other criteria, that 'your people believe their contribution to the organisation is recognised; that your organisation has a plan with clear aims and objectives which are understood by everyone, and your people understand how they contribute to achieving the organisation's aims and objectives'.

And what does their standard mean? IIP claims the standard 'sets out a level of good practice for training and development of people to achieve business goals'. Cynical employers know that the IIP logo in their reception and on their recruitment ads will attract good staff at lower wages because, 'It's not just the salary, it's the whole package.'

So. A quality standard that is supposed to highlight employers who respect their staff, is instead chased by companies eager to use it as an excuse to exploit their workers further. Sometimes you wonder if irony isn't redundant these days.

*James Pembroke*

# Jumping the Shark

'Jumping the shark' refers to the point at which a television or radio series makes a desperate bid to improve its ratings by introducing a melodramatic or fantastical plotline. From this point on, the series is usually doomed to failure.

The phrase was coined by Jon Hein at the University of Michigan back in the 1980s, and referred to an episode from *Happy Days*, the American comedy series, in which the lead character Fonzie literally tries to jump over a shark in a daredevil water-skiing stunt. For some of the audience, this was a leap too far.

American serials seem particularly adept at jumping the shark. Think of the infamous return of Bobby Ewing to *Dallas*, after he had been killed off several months earlier. So desperate were the producers to have Bobby back in the series that they were happy to dismiss all of season seven as Pam's dream. Legend has it that several alternative return-of-Bobby plotlines were filmed, including one that involved Bobby's evil twin. No wonder they went for the 'it was all just a bad dream' option.

More recent examples in the UK include the murder of Trevor Jordache in *Brookside* in the infamous 'body under the patio' storyline. Ratings soared for this episode, helped no doubt by the charms of Anna Friel as Beth Jordache (who was always going to be popular after the equally infamous lesbian kiss episode). But ever since Beth died in prison of a mysterious heart condition, the show's popularity appeared to wane dramatically, so much so that Channel 4 recently decided to axe it.

*Brookside* had broken the mould of serial drama when it was launched, with Channel 4 itself, in 1982. But gritty social realism should not be confused with sensationalism. Hard on the heels of the body under the patio came incest, petrol bombs and more lesbianism.

Similar melodrama followed *Brookside* creator Phil Redmond to the ITV soap, *Emmerdale Farm*. Having been brought on board to improve ratings, Redmond's revamp saw the dropping of 'Farm' from the programme's title and the introduction of spicier storylines, such as a Lockerbie-style plane crash in 1993, in which half the cast found their contracts terminated. More cast members were dispatched a few months later when a hostage-taking at the Post Office ended in a police shoot-out.

Ironically, as soap writers dream up increasingly sensational plotlines to retain audiences, so-called 'reality television' is pulling in the punters at an unimagined rate. It seems that many people are more interested in the mundane day-to-day existence of the *Big Brother* contestants or the working life of a flight attendant than in all the Sturm und Drang devised by drama writers. Which just goes to show that audiences can be infinitely fascinated by the everyday. The responsibility therefore lies with the writers, directors, producers and actors to tell the everyday well.

A record number of five million listeners tuned in to BBC Radio 4's *The Archers* at the end of 2002. And what was the storyline that had them so enthralled? Brian's affair with Siobhan. A standard soap storyline: the adulterous husband, the love-child, the oblivious wife and the younger lover. But like the best stories, it's a plot that can bear infinite repetition so long as it is well told. And not a dead body in sight.

Back in June this year, a man literally tried to jump a shark at Brighton's Sea Life Centre, by leaping naked into the shark tank for a £1 bet. The man emerged unhurt and ultimately escaped prosecution. The poor shark, however, died two days later, possibly due to stress. I'm sure there's a metaphor in there somewhere.

*Emma Harding*

**Modern tongue**

### Retail rages, No 1

- Clinically proven
  (by our own marketing department)
- Anti-ageing
- Up for grabs!

# Kippers

Are you now, or have you ever been, Kippered? Kippers is an acronym of Kids In Parents' Pockets Eroding Retirement Savings, and is a fast-rising sub-section of the population. Those charming young people, whom you lovingly and expensively nurtured and prepared for Life and then launched with a sigh of relief (however faint), have boomeranged and are now back in the nest, roosting.

Your feathers are ruffled: in Nature such behaviour is not tolerated. On reaching adulthood, young lions are chased out of the pride and expected to find, or even found, a pride of their own. Their presence threatens the status of the alpha male, who fears that the striplings will oust him and mate with his wives. This is not necessarily an immediate, let alone conscious, anxiety for the kippered father, but the analogy holds, in that he may well fear that energies which should now focus upon him are being diverted towards less deserving ends.

Kippered mothers have a slightly different take on the matter. The maternal instinct is legendary, and operates most powerfully when most needed, which is when the young are themselves powerless. But once they are fully equipped to fend for themselves, it seems only right and proper that they should do so. The fact that they do not arouses conflicting instincts of defence and attack. It's difficult to mature into a wise old matriarch while still complaining about the rim round the bath.

It's not as though the kippers themselves are any happier. Some of their early hopes have been dashed, the principal one being that of having their own habitat in which they can roam free and unchallenged, confidently marking their own territory. Many of them will have had a tantalising experience of independent living, and realise what they are missing. Their housemates at university or elsewhere largely shared their leisure interests, emotional temperature and hygiene standards. This is rarely the case under the parental roof, and however great the good will, both sides are apt to feel disenchanted. Family dynamics are in chaos and deep breaths must be drawn all round.

Because of the inexorable rise in house prices, unfeasibly large sums are tied up and unavailable for sharing out, so kippers are priced out of the market. They may well feel, 'It's so unfair!', and they are right. They hear their elders smugly recounting how they bought their delightful house in Camden Town in 1973 for less than the kipper's own derisory annual salary: no wonder they squat balefully, reverting to the kind of adolescent behaviour they purport to despise.

One of the compensations of the empty nest syndrome (once – inexplicably – dreaded) was that you didn't have to know about your children's hazardous activities, and could sleep in easy ignorance. Now you know, but cannot comment. I watched my 23-year-old kipper leaving the house on a dark, wet February evening. He unchained his bike, which I had only recently succeeded in forcing him to equip with a front light. He had forgotten his glasses, needed for distance. I said nothing. He did not have a helmet. I said nothing. But as he was about to wheel off, he reached into his jacket and produced his iPod. It was then that I cracked and said, 'Please don't put those earphones on!' He turned slowly round, paused, and said in a measured tone: 'Mum, you really do have to stop treating me like a child.'

Enraged, I embarked on a frenzy of displacement activity, often the only way to get dull chores under way. I descaled the iron, defrosted the fridge and put on a load of washing, including a pair of his jeans which I knew for a fact had not been washed since they were bought two years ago, and which were stiff with dirt. I now know, I really do now understand, that that was the whole point. Apparently they were vintage Levi's and now they are ruined, completely ruined. Not even the vagrants in the park would want to be seen dead in them. And I'm sorry. Very, very sorry. But they are clean now! And it would never have happened if I hadn't been kippered.

I consulted a friend whose kipper is unemployed. 'What are the upsides?' I begged. She had to think for quite a while, and eventually offered: 'Well, I do love the way he and his friends still want to change the world. And if the postman rings really loudly, he will take in parcels.'

*Flora Hinton*

## Kumbaya

*Kumbaya my Lord, Kumbaya*
*Kumbaya my Lord, Kumbaya*
*Kumbaya my Lord, Kumbaya*
*Oh Lord, Kumbaya*

They'd have you believe it was African. Well of course they would. Were it European, it would be merely maudlin, sub-literate, a parodic infantile whine for unspecified assistance, more appropriate to some ill-digested cargo cult than one of the most complex and mystical religions in the history of mankind.

But African, African is just fine. If 'Kumbaya' is African, then it's innocent, almost prelapsarian, noble in its simplicity, and, gosh darn it, moving – thousand upon thousand of black faces turned with child-like trust to the White Man come to lead them from benighted paganism into the Light of Christ, their eyes rolling ecstatically, their bodies swaying with that natural sense of rhythm, piccaninnies scrabbling in the dust . . . and so it plays beautifully into the lily-white, innately racist hands of the maundering classes.

And so they perpetuate the myth. A quick trawl around the world wide web produced, within ten seconds, this fine and juicy example: 'It originated in Africa among the native peoples who saw missionaries floating down the river in a boat. The natives were hungry to know about the Lord and they wanted the missionaries to "come by here", but their pronunciation made it sound like "Kum-by-ya". The words of the song are the natives' invitation to the Lord: "Come by here, my Lord, come by here"' (©1998 by Galen C. Dalrymple). (And, no, I am not making that up.)

Isn't that sweet? And isn't it touching that here and now, with all the advantages of two thousand years of Christendom, surrounded by the apparatus of our intelligence and sophistication, we can still become as little children each time the vicar – oops, Team Ministry Leader – Ken invites his good friend Roz to bring her guitar up to the sanctuary and strike up the drear, thudding chords of this, like, really meaningful song which, you know, would be a real favourite of Jezza's if He were here among us today, which in a very real sense He is . . .

*Someone's crying, Lord, Kumbaya;*
*Someone's crying, Lord, Kumbaya;*
*Someone's crying, Lord, Kumbaya;*
*O Lord, Kumbaya*

Someone? My money's on several million outraged African Christians, by and large a far more stern, orthodox, theologically unyielding and mystical bunch than any old rattle-bag of hangdog Western apologists; and one day they will rise up in a new Reformation, demanding a return to right thinking and decorum on the sanctuary and an end to patronising ethnocentricity. It will be the snake-pit for graspingly sentimental American fundamentalist preachers ('I prayed to Gawd! And Gawd! gave me a condo and a low mileage T-Bird and a 23-year-old helpmeet with candyfloss hair and big tits! And GAWD will do the same for YOU!') and the burning fiery furnace for the Holy Trinity Brompton crowd ('Jezza's having a drinks party, yah? and you're all invited to come, yah? I mean, doncha think Jezza's the most apsley brilliant chum?'); the guitars will be driven off the sanctuary, the laity will be flogged for desecrating the Host with unclean hands, and the acquiescent, favour-currying clergy will be driven into the sadomasochistic servitude they so richly deserve for having turned the church into a branch of New Labour.

And then will be the moment to reveal the truth about Kumbaya. African? Phooey. It's not African at all. It's not even anything to do with religion, let alone Jesus. Kumbaya is Welsh.

Yes. Would I lie? It's Welsh. Try it and you'll see what I mean, as in: 'Halloa, Mrs M, can you tell Griff to kumbaya on his way hoame and I'll give him that tinner paint he were after,' or 'I doan know what happened to our Lil, I told her to kumbaya but she musta gonbythur.' That an entire myth should have been built on such a simple misunderstanding is embarrassing; that millions of innocent, harmless worshippers should have had their liturgy disrupted with such inappropriate maunderings is lamentable; that the people of an entire continent should have been traduced by having it laid at their door is unforgivable.

*Michael Bywater*

## Life Coach

Life is hard. Life is a struggle. Life is a hard struggle punctuated by bouts of fear and uncertainty. Life is such a hard and uncertain fearful struggle that most of the time we're happy to keep our heads down, our aspirations low and our backside parked on the sofa.

Sometimes, we wonder what life might be like if we quit our jobs, followed our dreams, reached for the stars. But what with all the fear, struggle, uncertainty and whatnot sloshing around reminding us how difficult life is, we mostly decide that we're better off staying within our comfort zone, staying safe, staying on the sofa.

But maybe life needn't be like this. Maybe we really *can* do extraordinary things . . . Once this seed of dissatisfaction is planted, it eats away at you. But what to do about it? Call a life coach, that's what.

Having a life coach is a bit like being an athlete and having a sports coach, except instead of working with you to achieve better levels of fitness and performance in races and competitions, life coaches are coaching you towards a better performance in the race of life (sorry, once you begin spending time with life coaches, you start saying things like that).

It works like this: you tell them what you want to achieve in life (to have the courage to start your own company, or to write that novel, or whatever) and they help you achieve it. They do this by helping you address not only the practical issues involved in life changes (you want to start your own company? Then stop faffing around and go and talk to the bank manager), but also the emotional and psychological steps involved (have you procrastinated for years about starting your own company because you believe you won't be any good dealing with the finances? What can be done to change these beliefs?).

First off, you sign a contract agreeing to give 100 per cent effort, and together with your life coach you draw up a plan of action, with weekly goals to be met by you. Regular sessions are scheduled, which usually take place over the telephone, in order to monitor progress. You are responsible for doing all the running, with your coach providing the support and constructive advice and an endless stream of motivational claptrap such as 'There's no such thing as failure, only opportunities for personal growth.'

Life coaching homes in on a simple truth about modern living for the comfortably off: life is in fact neither hard, nor difficult, nor a struggle – it is merely that most people subscribe to a 'better the devil you know' attitude, fear change and lack faith in their own abilities. Life coaching subscribes to the view that, when challenged, people generally rise to the challenge and exceed expectations. (Life coaches are fond of citing the example of the role of the little ships at Dunkirk here.) It mixes this belief with a dash of elementary psychology (the power of positive thinking), a dose of common sense (time management), a smattering of self-help speak ('it is by spending yourself that you become rich'), and tops the lot off with what is surely coaching's most powerful weapon – namely that once you've paid someone else a king's ransom to believe in you, it would be a humiliating waste of time and money not to pull your finger out and go for it.

The examples of successful life coaching are too numerous to mention. Careers have been changed, lives turned around, ruts resoundingly got out of. You can even be your own life coach these days. Fiona Harrold, one of the UK's most successful life coaches (although you'd have to be suspicious of an under-achieving life coach, wouldn't you?), has published a book called *How To Be Your Own Life Coach*. It positively brims over with enthusiasm and self-esteem-enhancing case studies.

And although my cynical mind hates to admit it, life coaching is actually pretty hard to knock: OK, you can't help feeling that there's something a bit sad about paying a perfect stranger to tell you you're the greatest and give you a gentle kick up the arse, but if it brings about a demonstrable change in someone's life, then what's there to complain about?

Anyway, must finish here, as I'm off to step outside my comfort zone, embrace my fears as challenges, and get that dream job I've always wanted.

I've always really wanted to be a life coach.

*Nick Parker*

# McLabour

In Indonesia or Brazil, subverting the government costs a fortune. Ministers there know precisely how much they are worth, and buying them costs tens, sometimes hundreds of millions of dollars. This is money of the colour Lloyd George would have recognised. But corruption in Britain isn't what it used to be. Today, there's something rather shameful about the price for which the Government can be bought. Policy changes which have earned Bernie Ecclestone at least £400 million cost him a mere million, which was promptly returned to him the moment the Government's confidence in its own corruption faltered. During the conference season, Labour almost gives special access away.

For £15,000 McDonald's bought the rights to the most prestigious reception this year: the celebration of Labour's 100th party conference, attended by Tony Blair. For £10,000 you could buy the Government's question-and-answer session on education. Just £4,000 branded the video screen on which Mr Blair's speech was relayed. Democracy never came so cheap.

McDonald's said it would use the reception 'to talk about our community-based activities'. Presumably this does not include such community-based activities as undermining local cafés and restaurants, filling the streets with litter and making every town centre in Britain look the same. But at the McLabour conference, corporations could leave their reputations in the cloakroom.

Last year's fringe meeting on 'Tackling Financial Exclusion' was sponsored by Barclays, widely condemned for causing financial exclusion by shutting its smaller branches. The meeting on 'Creating a Savings Culture' was funded by Pearl, one of the companies named and shamed for damaging the savings culture by mis-selling pensions. The congress on 'Sustainability' was financed by Manchester Airport plc, whose new runway was condemned by Greens as one of the most destructive schemes ever built.

But, arguably, even the paltry sums required to fund these events are wasted, for McLabour has refined the art of anticipating corporate demands before they have even been made. Tony Blair's formula for winning the 1997 election was a simple one: wherever power existed already, he appeased it in the hope of acquiring some for himself.

Taking power meant capturing the heart of corporate Britain. And the corporations were ready to be seduced. They knew that the Tories would never defect, so a pro-corporate Labour Party meant that the electorate would be presented with a free and open choice between the party of big business and the party of big business. The corporate press, corporate donors, corporate power-brokers have deserted their old friends, who loved not wisely but too well.

The problem with appeasement is that it makes the people you appease more powerful. Big business is insatiable: however much you give it, it wants more. So the power of people and Parliament keeps rolling back, until democracy under McLabour starts to resemble the food in McDonald's: the packaging is rather more wholesome than the contents.

So, for all the spin about the People's Britain, whenever McLabour is confronted with a choice between what the electorate wants and what big business wants, it sides with big business. Look at the row over genetic engineering, for example, which split the only two constituencies Mr Blair cares about: Middle England and the corporations. Blair sided with the Addams Family firm, enraging Middle England. Look at the private finance initiative, which anyone except the idiots savants in the Treasury can see is a disastrous means of funding public services. Look at the rise of the supermarkets, whose economic cleansing of the food trade is almost complete. Look, if you can bear it, at Lord Haskins . . .

In McLabour's timid new world, everything is for sale. The tragedy is that it comes so cheap.

*George Monbiot*

# Micro-mobility

It has always seemed to me that the biggest problem with any British transport policy is that our options for personal transportation are exceptionally dull. In Italy, for example, it is law that you must spend your seventeenth year travelling everywhere by cappuccino-powered moped. In Holland, they had the entire country flattened by specially designed steamrollers in order to make it easier to cycle everywhere.

By contrast, Britain has the memory of the Sinclair C5. In 1985, Sir Clive Sinclair, inventor of the pocket calculator and a rubber-keyed computer, gave the world a grey, battery-powered go-kart that looked unsettlingly like a dismembered wheelie bin and was about as charming. It was so low to the ground that when driven on the roads people in cars didn't know you were there. (Although you knew perfectly well where they were, as you had a clear view down their exhaust pipes.) The AA condemned it as a serious risk to life expectancy. Luckily for the road fatality statistics, virtually nobody bought one. He tried again with the Zike in 1992 – a small-wheeled, battery-assisted bicycle which, he claimed, 'everyone will get off smiling'. It was unstable over potholes and riders found that it often had difficulty with hills. Very few people ever got on, let alone smiled.

But at least he tried. In this age of techno-this and dot-blah-that, where is the innovation? Something more than walking, something less than cycling, something to tide us over until scientists invent the personal jet-pack.

Well, I believe that something may well have arrived . . . As I was waiting for a train just a few weeks ago, a youth scooted – that is the only word for it, for that is what he was riding – down the platform on a tiny aluminium scooter, got off, flipped a latch on its shiny ergonomic body, folded it up into something small enough to fit into his rucksack, and got on the train. When we arrived at the end of the line, he flipped open his scooter again like an accessory on a Swiss army knife, and glided off through the crowds. He was riding a micro-skate scooter.

Stuff your integrated rail network, this was the transport revolution I had been waiting for. Before you could say the words 'Surely it's just an expensive children's toy, you fool?' I was micro-mobile. The blurb on the box had pictures of riders performing 'micro-manoeuvres' and extolled its virtues as an 'urban assault scooter', though this seemed to me to be protesting too much. (As well as plain nonsense: the chances of assaulting anything while scooting along on one leg are, frankly, slim.) This would make popping to the shops a dream, and that in itself was a noble aim.

Unlike rollerblades or skateboards, it does not require one to have exceptional balance or to wear ludicrous yoof clothing in order to operate. Yes, I do sometimes feel daft, weaving in and out of sensible people walking to work along the pavements, but the laconic hop that one has to do in order to power oneself along makes everyone smile. (They smile even more when I fall off . . .)

I am spotting more and more kindred scooter spirits. Sometimes we hail each other, as members of exclusive clubs are wont to do, even though it is difficult to steer and wave at the same time. Sometimes we exchange micro-gossip (I have recently learned of a fellow micro-oldie who ties her dogs to her scooter's handlebars and surfs water-ski style around Hyde Park.) And sometimes we just give thanks that a Swiss company thought up the micro-scooter first, and not Sir Clive Sinclair.

NB: For those who feel Sir Clive has been given a bit of a hard time here, please take solace from the fact that he currently markets the Zane II, a device that straps on to your regular bicycle and turns it into an electric one. On its first outing in front of the press in 1995, the prototype went backwards, although sales are now motoring steadily forwards, and cyclists who can't manage hills really, really like him.

*Nick Parker*

# Middle Youth

Age creeps up on us all. Often he is carrying a baseball bat, or at the very least a good sturdy garden spade. Then, at the moment we are least expecting it – during childbirth, perhaps, or halfway through being fired – he brings it down upon our heads with a giant clang. When we wake up our knees ache terribly, and all modern pop music sounds appalling. Cabinet ministers look younger, and we wonder whatever happened to pork luncheon meat. Age has crept up on us, the sly bastard.

This is why, I believe, so many people in their late thirties and forties keep turning around and looking behind them. Is he there yet? Can you see him out of the corner of your eye? When I was younger I assumed they were just worried about being overtaken by people like me, young, fleet of foot, sharp of eye, slim of thigh. As I have grown older, I have realised that young people are far less of a threat than they think they are, which is exactly the way it should be. No, in Middle Youth our main adversary is Age, and we are determined to keep him at bay.

Previous generations may not have known this was possible, or more likely just did not regard it as necessary. 'Act your age, not your shoe size,' as the diminutive pop star Prince once memorably observed. Instead of avoiding Age, people embraced him willingly, which is why all pre-war footballers looked forty-five and every police constable was at least fifty. Even the first beneficiaries of the great youth explosion of the fifties and sixties accepted the advance of Age. If you were middle-aged, you had, after all, survived, something a majority of previous generations hadn't quite managed. If this meant that in your time you came to loathe young people as fiercely as you had been loathed by your own elders, that was merely the natural order of things. You would have been as likely to wear a T-shirt after the age of forty as vote for Lordi in the Eurovision Song Contest. Assuming you even watched the Eurovision Song Contest, which of course you wouldn't have.

Somewhere along the line, however, middle age ceased to be a blessing and became an inconvenience. The categories muddied, and people became less interested in turning into their parents. Increasingly, the middle-aged stopped behaving in prescribed middle-aged fashions. With the job market contracting, and anyone who could remember Muffin the Mule seemingly destined for permanent unemployment, mid-life crises began earlier and went on for ever. Why embrace Age? What had he ever done for you?

So middle-aged people are putting off growing old for as long as possible. Some of them don't even want to grow up and, since no social phenomenon is too insignificant to be hijacked and exploited by marketing men, so Middle Youth was born. 'Act your shoe size, not your age,' as a recent ad for Clarks shoes had it.

Some Middle Youthers are not wolves in sheep's clothing, just sheep in lamb's clothing. They are ageing blokes in ill-fitting T-shirts driving tiny noisy sports cars with Radiohead on the in-car CD player. They are women with slightly broader smiles than they used to have, and much younger boyfriends. For them, Middle Youth is the last gasp: the view beyond is too horrible to contemplate.

Most Middle Youthers, however, do not need to recapture their youths, as they never let go of them in the first place. They just do what they always did – wear the same clothes, listen to the same music, have the same ridiculous drunken conversations and fall out of bed at the weekend with far worse hangovers. Their least favourite line of the Bible is 'When I was a child, I spake as a child, I understood as a child, I thought as a child; but when I became a man, I put away childish things.' Why? they whine. Who said we have to? It's not fair!

The only problem is that Age is still out there, in the shadows, his garden spade at the ready. We can't look over our shoulders for ever. Our concentration only has to waver for a second, and CLANG! he has got us again. Still, at least he's not carrying a scythe. Yet.

*Marcus Berkmann*

# Nature Identical Flavourings

If a scientist analyses a strawberry, works out which chemicals give it its taste, then synthesises those chemicals in a lab, there is no difference whatsoever between the 'natural' and 'artificial' versions. You couldn't tell them apart.

Yet Modern Folk believe that there is a difference, which is why they have to be coddled with phrases like 'nature identical'. It's partly snobbery; 'artificial' things are made by horrible common scientists in fluorescent-lit labs: beastly men with Adam's apples, who wear stiff tweed from Dunn & Co with cheap pens in the top pockets and have wives called Marjorie And The Kiddies.

It is also in part a primitive belief in magic, the same belief that infects PR men, corporate image consultants and politicians: the belief that naming something gives one power over its qualities. Both the man who buys a bottle of cheap scent because it is called Phallus and the politician who speaks of 'green shoots' believe, like wizards or alchemists, that by pronouncing something, they can become it.

This nature business is particularly sad and silly. Not only can you not become 'natural' by buying a packet with the word 'nature' on it, but the very image of nature these gulls have is wrong and lethal. They envisage a tranquil and untouched Eden, unspoilt by the works of man: a 'nature' which would not support them for a month unless it were subdued, raped and made to bring forth its fruits. It is as bizarre a fantasy as any of Capability Brown's artificial wildernesses. The truth of 'nature' is that it has become yet another laboratory, manipulated not by gnarled and timeless Peter Mayle-style peasants with rank armpits and a profound knowledge of life, death and the cycle of the seasons, but by men in suits and poly-cotton shirts, sitting by the silos in their company Sierras punching the revised yield-per-hectare estimates into their Blackberries.

The point has been often made that the modern obsession with 'nature', expressing itself in such heterogeneous weirdness, gullibility and *schweinerei* as Body Shop banana-flavoured hair putty, didgeridoos, ley lines, song-lines, Glastonbury and vibes, is fundamentally an urban and profoundly sentimental fantasy. If it ever escaped from the gaudy theme-park of the young, privileged Western mind and became the basis of a real culture, it would lead to mass death from malnutrition and disease.

*Michael Bywater*

## Neuromarketing

You have signed on the dotted line. A smartly dressed woman, who looks more like a TV executive than a scientist, smiles at you and explains what is about to happen. You lie down obediently, a button is pressed and you slide gently into the coffin-like tube. It's a little claustrophobic, but you like to be helpful. The team retire to an adjoining observation room. You are excited, apprehensive – what will they find out about you? After all, you are giving them access to your innermost regions, your greyest matter, in a procedure as invasive as the most intimate examination.

You lie in the white tube, looking up at a mirror. The smart woman's voice comes over the intercom. 'I'm going to show you some images,' she says, 'and I want you to imagine yourself using them.' The slide show begins: a can of Pepsi, a white-sanded Caribbean beach, a cruiser convertible, the actress Anna Friel, a cuddly toy. You are reminded briefly of *The Generation Game*.

Eventually, the slide show ends and you emerge from the tube. You are shown a computer screen with your brain in slices. The smart woman points in triumph at a yellow dot near the top of the brain – the medial prefrontal cortex. Activity here means that a consumer isn't deliberating over a product, he's ready to buy. His credit card is already burning a hole in his faded Levis.

You gaze at the yellow blobs in wonder and embarrassment. Your brain has given away your deepest, darkest impulses. Now they know, these scientists, that you long to drive that cruiser convertible with Anna Friel at your side. You are thanked for your co-operation and your data is added to the file.

This is neuromarketing – the employment of technology such as functional Magnetic Resonance Imaging (fMRI) to monitor brain activity in response to commercial products or advertising. The notion is so captivating that several major companies are now investing serious money in research. They believe that the electrical impulses in our brains will tell them everything they need to know about human desire and decision-making, enabling them to tweak and target their products accordingly.

The medial prefrontal cortex is the part of the brain commonly associated with our sense of self. If a product or image causes electrical activity here, it's probably because that product or image corresponds to our own sense of who we are. And this kind of information is gold dust to a company with a product to sell.

Until now, focus groups have formed the bedrock of product marketing, but they are subject to some of the basic flaws in human psychology. We often don't know our own minds and we can also feel pressured to say what we imagine people want to hear. The journey from brain to mouth is not always straightforward. But a brain scan provides a snapshot of thought in action – and the brain never lies.

Car manufacturers Ford and DaimlerChrysler have both carried out neuromarketing pilots. DaimlerChrysler has formed a research group called MindLab with the University Clinic of Ulm in Germany, where projects have included a study of how men react to certain car designs. Predictably, the cars that lit up most male brains were at the sports end of the range, but the scientists also managed to identify the part of the brain activated by these images. This was the right ventral striatum, the part of the brain associated with reward and the area that is also stimulated by sex, drugs and chocolate.

Protest groups have already started to question whether neuromarketing research is medically ethical. Others have criticised the use of medical technology for marketing purposes. Recently, a group of psychologists asked Emory University in Atlanta to call a halt to their neuromarketing experiments, saying that they were likely to be used 'to promote disease and human suffering'.

But what brain scans still can't predict is human behaviour. They can't follow the thought process that occurs between the activation of desire – a naked Anna Friel convincing you of your need for a certain mobile phone during the commercial break in *Coronation Street* – and the concrete act of making that purchase. Recording mental responses is one thing, but it's when neuromarketeers finally work out how to manipulate brain processes themselves that we really have to worry.

*Emma Harding*

# Parkour

Open a map of your home town. Draw a straight line from A to B. Imagine travelling between these two points just as your straight line dictates, without considering the elements in your way as obstacles (houses, buildings, fences, trees, railings, barriers). Jump over or under them, climb, roll, run. This is Le Parkour, as explained on the UK Parkour website, Urban Freeflow.

Founded by Frenchman David Belle and his friend Sébastian Foucan, Parkour, or 'Free Running', is classed as an 'extreme urban sport'. Using the urban environment that surrounded them in the concrete estates of the Paris suburbs where they lived, Belle, Foucan and others developed a philosophy of movement that involves daredevil jumps and rolls across the gaps between buildings, and seemingly death-defying gymnastics as they clamber up bridges, buildings and just about anything else that confronts them. Traceurs (those who participate in Parkour) are like real-life spidermen. Mistakes can easily lead to accidents, sometimes fatal. Concrete is not known for being a particularly forgiving surface to fall on to.

Belle and Foucan see Parkour as allied with the discipline and strength found in martial arts, as well as with the principles of George Herbert, the inventor of the 'méthode naturelle' of physical education. Around the time of the First World War, Herbert was struck by the physical development of the indigenous peoples he saw in Africa – 'Their bodies were splendid, flexible, nimble, skilful, enduring, resistant and yet they had no other tutor in Gymnastics but their lives in Nature.' Herbert developed a theory of physical education which made great use of obstacle courses, using the 'ordinary things in life' as obstacles. Belle and Foucan have taken his ideas further, using instead the obstacles found in an urban environment – the jungles of Africa transposed to the concrete jungle.

But isn't it all just old-fashioned running around a bit, with added cod spiritualism? When we went climbing trees, did we feel the need to call it 'rural freeflow' and witter on about how the 'ascent of the branches was akin to man's journey through life'? No, of course we didn't. Everything's got to be a bloody *lifestyle choice* these days.

Still, it's nice to see that at least a few people wearing tracksuits and trainers around town are actually putting them to some use.

*Sonali Chapman*

# Pashmina

There is only one certainty in the fickle world of high fashion. When a once-exclusive item of couture chic becomes available on the high street, it ceases to be desirable to the fashion elite, who then have to go to more extreme lengths to keep ahead of the pack. The story of pashmina shawls is a shining example of this fashion truth.

'Pashmina' is the Persian word for cashmere and has come to be synonymous with the large, soft, silk-and-cashmere shawls which for hundreds of years were a luxury item amongst India's elite. Once draped over the shoulders of only the richest women in India, pashminas are now worn all over the world.

While most travellers in Asia pick up nothing more exotic than a tie-dye T-shirt and a stomach bug, somebody on their travels must have spotted a pashmina shawl, for one made its way back to Europe, where it was spotted by Sophia Swire. Being fashionably inclined (and presumably also filthy rich), she bought a load for herself and her friends. One of her friends was spotted sporting hers by the fashion editor of *Vogue*, and soon a pashmina shawl was the accessory. For a few golden years the pashmina set swanned around Europe, an exclusive in-crowd garnering comments from all they met about the softness, luxuriousness and all-round splendidness of their elegant shawls. But fashion critical mass was reached, and the shawls inevitably found their way into the mass market. Now it is impossible to walk down your local high street without bumping into hordes of pashmina-clad women.

Funnily enough, bumping into things is something that pashmina wearers must be familiar with, as it appears that the art of elegantly draping a pashmina over one's shoulders eludes the majority of the fashion sheep, who usually knot their shawls tightly around their necks like football scarves, leaving them to stagger round wearing furry pastel neck braces. Just as Volvo drivers have a reputation for being the worst drivers, so you would be well advised to avoid those who wear pale-pink pashminas. Not merely because they might collide with you as they stagger round half-throttled by their shawls, but also because who wants to be seen around those who can't dress properly, darling?

But what of the poor fashionistas, their once exclusive shawls now garrotting half the nation? Where were they to find a shawl that was softer, rarer and altogether more chic? They found it in shatoosh. Shatoosh is mouse-brown in its undyed colour, so gossamer-like that it is said a whole shawl can be drawn through a wedding ring, and amazingly rare, due to the fact that it is supposedly spun from the chin hair of the Himalayan chiru antelope, collected by hand from where it has snagged on the thorny bushes of the Tibetan plateau, and transported by pack mule to Nepal.

Unfortunately, this story is a myth: shatoosh is made from the soft winter undercoat of the chiru, which is no less scarce than beard hair but a good deal more prosaic, as the only way to separate it from the chiru is to kill them, and you have to kill an awful lot of chiru just to make one scarf. In the last fifty years, the population of Tibet's chiru has shrunk from countless millions to less than 75,000, many of them caught and left to die in leg-hold traps; although there have been reports of entire herds being machine-gunned in the Qinghai region of Tibet. Which is why trade in shatoosh is illegal, and why unscrupulous dealers make more than $6,000 per shawl on the black market.

Let's hope they choke in unfortunate scarf-tieing accidents.

*Nick Parker*

*'And now a look at tomorrow's front pages – the Telegraph leads with "Ultimate Makeover Guide", while the Mail has "A Fantastic New You" . . .'*

# Personal Grooming

Are you groomed? I mean, are you *groomed*? I bet you're not. Not like I am. I am lethally groomed. If you saw me in the street, you would probably say, 'Who is that incredibly groomed man?'

At least, that is what I would like to think. The probability is that you would not even notice. You wouldn't see the anguish, the expense, the time, the sheer pressure on storage space which lies behind my astoundingly commonplace appearance. But I know, you see. I can look at myself and think: 'What would I look like, were I not so comprehensively groomed?' And I know the answer. I'd look exactly the same.

This grooming, you see, is a racket. I know just how much of a racket it is because I have completely fallen for it. My bathroom shelf is a monument to grooming. There's the Clinique Scruffing Lotion, the Clinique Facial Scrub, the Clinique Body Scrub and the Clinique Oil-Free Moisturiser. There's also the Basic Homme Daily Cellular Renovator, the Aramis Lab Series Anti-Ageing Supplement, the Kiehl All-day Moisturiser and the Biotherm Active Anti-Fatigue. That is just part of my skin grooming department. Then there is hair. I have my Klorane Cantaureas shampoo, my Kiehl Creme with Silk Groom, my Kiehl conditioner, my Flex conditioner, my Penhaligon's Florimelle and my Trumper's department: Eucris, Floreka (green and amber, to be on the safe side), Coronis and San Remo. Passing on to the scent section, there are Bois de Portugal, Erolfa and Green Irish Tweed, from Creed of Paris; Vanille, Lavande Créole, Voleur des Roses and Eau de Navigateur, from Jean Laporte; Hammam from Penhaligon's; and Acqua di Colonia Russa, from the Officinali Farmaceutica di Santa Maria Novella in Florence.

These are the things which are on the shelf. There are other things in the cupboards but I dare not look.

Sometimes I think of my grandfather's bathroom. In my grandfather's bathroom, there was:

1) Palmolive.
2) Erasmic shaving soap.
3) Violet hair tonic, sometimes.

My grandfather could give you good reasons for having these things. Palmolive got him clean. Erasmic shaving soap softened his beard. Violet hair tonic stopped his hair sticking up if he was going somewhere special. If he was just seeing patients, he didn't use it. All his patients knew his hair stuck up anyway.

I cannot give you good reasons for my stuff, except that I am some kind of sucker. I think I have worked out what sort of sucker I am, but let us leave that for a moment while we look at the common or garden sucker, as manipulated in the glossy magazines aimed at lethally groomed man. This sort of sucker hasn't a clue. He is probably between twenty and thirty-five years old and is not in a job he particularly likes, although he is dreadfully ambitious about it. He is aware that, in most particulars of life, he fails to meet the Mills & Boon specifications for romantic hero. His peregrinations are confined to the daily trip to work and back. If he goes abroad, it is on business, surrounded by other businessmen in the same suit, carrying the same briefcase, and using the same pen to write the same preposterous 'sales projections' in the same notepad (Soft Burnished Executive Leather).

Inside, though, he knows that what women really want is a rugged, bushwhacking sort of fellow with devil-may-care blue eyes and the lithe, sardonic grace of the panther stalking its kill. Alternatively, they want one of these French johnnies with sensitive features, soulful eyes, a sardonic half-smile and a fifteenth-century château. Either way, sardonic is important. Our man does not possess and cannot acquire those dubious virtues. So, instead, he buys products which are advertised by presenting the image of a male model dressed up to look as if he does possess those characteristics. It requires a prodigious gullibility on the part of our little chap, but it nevertheless works.

I am looking at an advert for something called Jazz, a perfume for men. The ad shows models – two men and a woman – wearing expensive suits, striding up a street in San Francisco at dawn. One man has his arm round the woman. The other has his tie loosened and is loping along with a sardonic smile. They are all pretending to be happy and successful and having fun. Indeed, the subtlety of the ad is in its suggestion that you can have this sort of Big Fun even if you don't have a girlfriend.

It is a great, shining, trumpeting scam, the whole thing. It is selling images to the insecure. It is the illusion of a chimera seen in a mirage. It is ultimately unkind, for it offers hope where there is none.

It is also profoundly silly. There is a clear rule that you should not be able to smell someone's scent beyond arm's length; and yet images like this suggest that the scent will bring them in range from across a crowded room. No. Too much scent repels, on men even more than on women. It is selling the oldest trick in the world: Buy me and your life will be different.

I would never buy a male grooming product on the strength of an advertisement offering me a different life. I like to think I have overladen my shelves with things of inherent merit, and, if you let me, I will bore you stupid on top notes, fixatives and woody accords; on the harmony of vanilla and lavender, of moss and tonquin.

But I also think that I, too, am trying to buy an image. It's just that the image that I buy says: 'Here is a man who is not fooled by advertisement.'

It is an irksome conundrum, and one which will only be solved by an act of will. I must embrace asceticism, throw my balms and ointments into a black plastic bag, and deck my bathroom like a cell. Palmolive. Erasmic shaving soap. Violet hair tonic for special occasions. Then what will my grooming ritual say about me?

It will say: 'Here is a man who washes and shaves when he gets up.' But is that enough? Will women gaze after me in the street, and men gnash their teeth with envy? I long for the day when I no longer give a damn.

*Michael Bywater*

**Modern tongue**

### Retail rages, No 2

- Because you're worth it
- Classic
  (When used to describe things that are just normal, like calling ready-salted a 'classic flavour'.)
- Limited edition flavours
  (Only twelve million lemon-flavoured jaffa cakes made this week . . .)

## Piped Music

According to a 1997 *Sunday Times* poll, when people were asked what was 'the single thing they most detested about modern life', piped music came third on the list. I'd like to think it's moved up since then, as piped music, or CAN – 'captive audience network', as it's officially called – has become even more ubiquitous, making life near-intolerable in restaurants, pubs, cafés, foyers, swimming pools, gyms, shops (posh shops and cheap shops, including most bookshops), hairdressers, hospitals' and doctors' waiting rooms, airports and aeroplanes and now, I can hardly believe it, BANKS: intolerable to anyone with any hearing left, who still likes to choose their own music or likes silence (or even just a quiet chat).

My bank has recently installed piped music in its branches. When I complained to the manager, she said that they had done a survey amongst their customers who had overwhelmingly agreed that piped music alleviates the boredom of standing in line and makes them feel less anxious about the anticipated consultation with the bank clerk. What did we do before piped music? I asked her, but by her expression I realised that she hadn't been around then and couldn't imagine what we did in a quiet bank. I've banked with them for over thirty years but I can no longer talk to a real person on the phone at the bank, so I'm planning to end the relationship in silent bitterness and fury. I feel like André Previn who, apparently, was on board an aircraft during an emergency, and when the pilot piped 'soothing' music through the plane's public address system, he complained to the stewardess saying, 'I refuse to die to this music'.

Some people are benefiting, however. It seems that interminable loops of the same music earn the Performing Rights Society over £242 million a year because every outlet must have a licence from them. That means that every meal we eat, book we buy, service we use has an extra cost attached to it from this near-universal modern scourge.

Piped music is unchosen by customers and, in many cases, they cannot prevent it. I have often begged the people serving me in bookshops or restaurants to turn it off or down, only to be told it's impossible as it's on a system which the 'global owners' have insisted on and paid for. I'm not sure whether that's just an excuse but it may be true of the chains. Small independent shops can create their own music loops from iPods and the Internet, but you're still being forced to listen to someone else's choice of music, usually played so loud you can't think or talk.

There is a wonderful organisation called Pipedown campaigning against this thing. When you join them for a very small amount of money (£15 a year), they send you small cards you can hand out to places where you've hated the muzak intrusion and won't be coming back, or other small cards where you've noticed that there's a glorious silence and you want to thank the establishment. It's supported by several musicians – Alfred Brendel, Simon Rattle, Gillian Weir etc. – as well as actors, writers and broadcasters, and thousands of others around the country, although I'm afraid that I didn't spot any young pop musicians on their list of patrons.

When I was young, my parents sang and played, and taught us to sing for ourselves: 'the songs came from our own lips, not out of a box,' as Flora Thompson puts it. It feels as if singing for ourselves, and not just listening to others, has been stolen from us by the electrical music industry, and all we have left is karaoke – which, I see from the *OED*, is from the Japanese meaning 'empty orchestra'.

- Pipedown can be contacted at 1 The Row, Berwick St James, Salisbury SP3 4TP

*Jean McCrindle*

*'Margery – it's your life coach.'*

# Pokémon

The trouble with some aspects of modern life is that they are so complex only small children can understand them. The Pokémon phenomenon is an example. I will try my best, I will go slowly, but remember, this isn't like understanding how the futures markets work, it's far trickier than that. If you get stuck, a grandchild might be able to help, once he's finished setting the video.

Pokémon (translation: 'Pocket Monsters') started life as a computer game for the Nintendo Game Boy (a pocket-sized computer console). The object of the game was to catch the 150 different Pokémon, train them and then use them to fight opponents in a bid to become 'the greatest Pokémon trainer of all time'. Pokémon is a cross between a tamagotchi (electronic pet that lives in a key ring) and conkers. The game has been enormously successful in Japan and has subsequently taken off across the globe. Pokémon characters can now be found on everything that your average ten-year-old can play with, wear or stuff in his mouth.

But the Pokémon story is no ordinary tale of breathtakingly-cynical-product-placement-and-market-saturation, for under the motto of 'Gotta Catch 'Em All', Pokémon may well have attained the Holy Grail of children's marketing: the toy that you have to keep on buying.

This stroke of genius started with the original Pokémon computer game, of which there are three different versions, each almost identical, except that each has a handful of 'unique' Pokémon characters. So in order to 'Catch 'Em All' you either have to buy the other versions (£35 each) or 'trade' them with other players, by linking your Game Boys up with a cable (£7.99, available exclusively from Nintendo, naturally). Pokémon is like a game of conkers in which every player has to own his own horse-chestnut tree and then buy his bits of string from a licensed string dealer.

While the world's children were busy zapping away on their Game Boys, Nintendo developed the Pokémon Trading Card Game, basically an elaborate game of snap in which the game itself is merely an excuse for buying more and more cards. Page 2 of the Trading Card Game rule-book plugs the TV shows. Page 3 plugs *The Duellist*, '. . . one of the leading trading card game magazines, to be found at most larger newsstands'. Page 4 tells you how to spot rare and valuable cards and advises that 'First Editions' are difficult to 'catch' ('buy'). It is not until Page 5 that you are told how to play the game. New cards are added to the repertoire all the time, at over £7 per pack. It is the only card game I know of where each player has to own his own deck of cards in order to play.

But in order not to be seen to be resting on its laurels (those would be exclusive Pokémon laurels, you understand, and any resting™ would have to be in accordance with special resting™ rules available only at larger branches of Toys 'R' Us), Pokémon employs one final pocket-money-draining tactic, previously employed by the makers of Beanie Babies (small bean-filled cuddly toys that you buy for £3 and sell for £3,000): announcing the 'retirement' of certain product ranges. Under the banner of 'Catch 'Em While They're Still Available', Hasbro, the makers of the Pokémon collectible action figures, frequently discontinue certain specific makes, creating instant demand which sends prices soaring. If we were talking about shares and not bendy bits of rubber, this practice would be called insider dealing.

In the dystopian future of Aldous Huxley's *Brave New World*, the Director of the breeding programme surveyed his children playing 'Centrifugal Bumble-Puppy', a game which involved one of the children throwing a ball into a complex and expensive machine which whirred and spun and finally spat the ball back randomly for one of the other children to catch. 'Strange', mused the Director, '. . . to think that even in Our Ford's day most games were played without more apparatus than a ball or two and a few sticks and perhaps a bit of netting. Imagine the folly of allowing people to play elaborate games which do nothing whatever to increase consumption'.

Centrifugal Bumble-Pokémon™ will soon be in a toyshop near you, no doubt.

*Nick Parker*

# Psychometrics

Psychometric testing – multiple-choice or short-answer questions, with standardised conditions and methods of scoring – was first introduced in France at the beginning of the last century and used extensively during both world wars for quickly processing the millions of conscripted soldiers and assigning them to relevant ranks and jobs. Over the last ten years, however, it has become almost synonymous with 'candidate selection' by large corporations.

On one level psychometrics benefits both candidates and companies – basic numeracy and literacy tests can weed out unsuitable applicants who might have been able to use the gift of the gab to get through a traditional interview, while well-suited candidates who are nervous or tongue-tied in front of the panel stand a better chance if their test results reflect their true potential. However, alongside testing objective skills there has recently been a significant growth in personality-based psychometric testing, supposedly designed to assess a candidate's psychological suitability for the job in question. These tests are a kind of pop psychoanalysis, and are of extremely dubious worth.

In the interests of research I took a psychometric test under 'candidate conditions'. Here I was asked to respond by selecting two of the following statements, marking one 'most true' and another 'least true':

*I am the sort of person who:*

- Has a lot of new ideas
- Feels calm
- Likes to understand things
- Is easy to get on with

Actually, all the above could be said to apply to me, though being easy to get on with and having lots of new ideas were probably the most relevant. (Although how many ideas count as 'lots'? And are we talking original pieces of thought or just random musings such as 'I wonder what Branston pickle tastes like with cornflakes?') As I am only allowed to choose one statement as 'most true', I opt for being easy to get on with.

And then I change my mind. In a fit of panic I remember that this isn't some 'just for fun' personality test in a teen magazine – it is for a job! Here I am saying that the most important thing about me is that I am relaxed and chatty and you'd probably quite like me if you met me at a cocktail party! I change my answer to the 'new ideas' option, Definitely the most important thing about me is that I am a creative powerhouse, churning out at least fifteen original philosophical concepts every hour. If this doesn't single me out as the man for the job, I don't know what will.

Phew. So what am I going to pick as 'least true'? I study the list again and decide that choosing 'Likes to understand things' would not be clever ('Yes, I'd like this job because I think it really suits they way I like to stumble through life in a fog of ignorance and denial'). So I plump for 'Feels calm'. Which is ridiculous because I am a very calm person, and now I'm painting a picture of myself as an edgy, nervous neurotic. Oh dear.

There are nineteen other questions on the same lines, through which I impart the knowledge that 'I enjoy organising events', 'have lots of energy', 'develop new approaches' and 'sometimes get angry'.

My own mother wouldn't recognise me.

Candidates quickly learn how best to answer the questions to display what is required. Big corporations try to counteract this by modifying the tests, but I suspect that they're not really bothered one way or the other – the reason that human resources departments really love psychometric tests is because they lend an air of pseudo-scientific efficiency to the interview process, as well as giving them something to blame if their candidate turns out to be a dud. ('We can't work out why Mr Parker was such a miserable sod in the office – his profile said he was going to be a really easy-going guy.')

*Nick Parker*

# Reality TV

Who was it that said humankind was unable to bear very much reality? T. S. Eliot, of course, possibly after watching the umpteenth series of *Taxicab Confessions* or *Who Wants to Marry My Dad?* But unfortunately he was dead wrong. The universal popularity of 'reality' TV shows no signs of abating. At least 200 shows are listed on the US website 'Reality TV World', where news flashes include 'Former *Average Joe* star Adam Mesh gets married' and 'New *Apprentice* winner Sean Yazbeck clarifies he's not engaged.' The only cheerful development advertised on this generally rather depressing noticeboard is the exciting news that there's to be a 'feline mini reality show' on the Animal Planet network called *Meow Mix House*, which will involve the bold pretence that ten rescue cats, living together in a purpose-built 'house', could each give a damn about what the other nine are doing.

Reality TV all started off with *Candid Camera* in 1948. Not many people know that the veteran Buster Keaton took part in stunts for *Candid Camera*, sitting alongside bored bobby-soxers in small-town diners and then dropping his hat in his soup, while the camera filmed the nervous giggling. Overnight, a new kind of prurient entertainment was born, and it has grown and grown. There are now various genres – none of them with much claim to 'reality' – that come under the umbrella heading of 'reality TV'. First, there is the 'docusoap', pioneered by BBC producer Paul Watson with *The Family* in 1974 and continued through series such as *Airport* and *Driving School*, where real people are observed by 'fly on the wall' camera crews, and become famous in the process. Then there are 'special living environment' shows, such as *Big Brother*, or *Castaway*, or *The 1900 House* (these sometimes have gladiatorial game-show aspects); then make-over programmes of various sorts; celebrities allowing cameras to document their lives (*The Osbournes*); and job-search programmes such as *The Apprentice*. Other kinds of programme that are sometimes counted as 'reality' are talent shows such as *Pop Idol* or *Strictly Ballroom Dancing*.

Most of these shows are plainly addictive; once a viewer makes the decision to watch the new series of *Big Brother*, for example, there is evidently no way out but death. Personally, I have watched *Big Brother* only once: the first 'celebrity' series, which lasted just one week, and was done for the BBC's Comic Relief. It featured Jack Dee, Anthea Turner, Vanessa Feltz and others – and over those short few days I certainly discovered I was not immune to the format. Far from it, in fact: I got dangerously involved – voting repeatedly to get rid of that vain git from Boyzone; talking about *Big Brother* incessantly to people who weren't watching it; losing all sense of proportion about what a terrific chap Jack Dee was. Astonishingly, I even dreamed about it (twice). But at the end of that week, I was not proud of myself. Because, yes, there is no denying that the *Big Brother* format appeals to something very basic in the human psyche. But, as all sorts of notorious psychological experiments have proved over the years, there are many, many cruel things basic to the human psyche that are better left undisturbed.

Prurience is the main appeal of reality TV. From the craven safety of one's own sofa, one can watch a group of 'real' people operating under conditions of artificial pressure. This is bound to be fascinating, from a sociological point of view, but it is basically exploitative – and it cuts no ice at all that the participants are aware of the exploitation, have volunteered for it, and have been specially selected for their robust personalities. These participants sometimes even fondly imagine they are in control, but they're always wrong. Everyone is being manipulated by the makers of the programme – especially the audience, which incidentally gets the same message, time after time, that 'real' people are almost ferally self-interested, and will do absolutely anything to be famous. One of the worrying side-effects of reality TV is that, for television viewers, there is now almost no separation between the notions of celebrity and self-abasement. Public self-abasement is seen as the principal path to fame; meanwhile famous people must abase themselves on television as often as possible, because it is the wish of the mob.

Of course, in this world of post-modern irony, there have now been 'spoof' reality shows, too – such as Channel 4's *Space Cadets*, in which some of the participants were 'real', while some were actors in on the joke (the joke was that the cadets weren't really going into space). At the extreme, *Truman Show* end of the spectrum, an American series called *The Joe Schmo Show* featured just one real person surrounded by actors pretending to be reality TV show participants – and astonishingly, the real chap didn't sue them afterwards for existentialist trauma; instead, apparently, he was quite proud of his catch-phrase, 'What's going *on*?' Yes, the nightmare imaginings of Franz Kafka are now routinely offered up for mainstream entertainment. And they wonder why some of us are so doomy.

On the plus side, no one has actually murdered anyone yet in a reality show, but it's only a matter of time. Maybe it will happen first in the Meow Mix House! However, I just watched for a few minutes on the webcam, and all that happened was that a large white cat, with its paws crossed, moved its head a bit. Interestingly, in 1968, the TV playwright Nigel Kneale predicted the whole reality TV thing in his dystopian BBC play *The Year of the Sex Olympics* (starring Leonard Rossiter) – but, although that's a fascinating fact, it's of no consolation whatsoever.

*Lynne Truss*

# Retail Anthropologist

Shopping used to be a chore. It was restocking the larder or replacing things that were worn out. It was drudgery and inconvenience and a stand-up row every time you wanted a refund. Now you only have to look at one of the new shopping malls, like Bluewater in Kent, to realise that shopping has become our number one leisure activity. Our obsession with shopping has fuelled a retail explosion, with more and more companies selling vast amounts of competing products to increasingly discerning customers. It is no longer enough to pile 'em high and sell 'em cheap. The battle for our business has moved from our wallets and purses to our hearts and minds: if companies are going to retain us as customers they have to get under our skin – they are going to need a science of shopping. They are going to need retail anthropology.

Envirosell, a company set up by a Mr Paco Underhill, 'urban geographer and retail anthropologist', has been developing such a science for nearly twenty years. Like all good anthropologists, his chief source of data is his subject in its natural habitat – the shopper shopping. Armed with time-lapse cameras, video recorders and 'trackers' with clipboards, retail anthropologists will trail shoppers and document their every move. How many products touched, how many labels read, which aisles cruised, which signs ignored, which products surreptitiously opened and sampled in preference to the sampler provided . . . the bacteria in your average Petri dish don't enjoy such scrutiny.

So if you're thinking of opening a shop, or marketing a product, you would do well to bear some of their findings in mind. If you are a mere shopper, then it is as well to know your enemy . . .

There is a 'transition zone' at the front of stores. Retailers had previously thought that the best position for their wares was at the front, but when people enter a shop they adjust their walking pace, accustoming themselves to the change in light levels, acclimatising themselves to the new sights and sounds. Put anything within 10 to 15 feet of a doorway and customers will walk right past it.

People unconsciously quicken their pace when walking past banks. Don't open a shop next to a bank, as people will be too busy hurrying past the bricks-and-mortar reminder of their overdraft to pay any attention to your wares.

Mirrors are good though. We can't resist looking at ourselves in mirrors and preening like chimps. A mirror placed by a display will slow people down, and they are more likely to take a look.

Eighty-six per cent of women look at price tags when they shop, compared to only seventy-two per cent of men. For a man, ignoring the price tag is almost a measure of his virility.

Sixty-five per cent of men who try something on will buy it. Only twenty-five per cent of women will. Make it easier for men to get to the changing rooms and they'll practically throw their money at you.

An American supermarket that had failed to stop gangs of youths loitering in its car parks after hours, in spite of fences and security guards, was advised just how style-conscious yoof was: it piped Mantovani over a loud-speaker system, and the gangs moved on. It was just too uncool to hang out to the strains of easy listening.

Why should we care? Surely this is just another example of a calculating modern world trying to screw us out of our cash. True, there will no doubt always be those who exploit us as we shop – pumping the smell of freshly baked bread through the air conditioning to give a false impression of wholesomeness, or deceitfully packaging their wares to confuse the unwary shopper (Sunny Delight is not a fresh fruit juice, even though it is kept in the chiller cabinets; Farm Fresh eggs are just battery-farmed eggs with pictures of happy chickens on the boxes) – but the Science of Shopping is on the whole going to prove good news, especially for oldies. As we make up an ever-increasing percentage of the population, businesses are having to pay closer attention to our needs and desires. And as the retail anthropologists have far too many videotapes of oldies not bothering to stoop for products on awkward shelves, or putting products back because they can't read the tiny type on the boxes, change cannot be far away. The hour of the Grey Pound may soon be upon us.

*Nick Parker*

## Retail Motivator

A new person is becoming fashionable in the highly competitive world of the High Street. She – and it is more likely to be a she – is seen to be the answer to big stores or chains that have flagging sales, bored shop assistants and shops devoid of customers.

Worried that they could go under to better-placed competitors, the firm's human resources division (once more humbly known as the boring personnel department) sends for the retail motivator. Like many things in Britain today she is an American invention, someone over there who is now coming over here. A cross between an Evangelical preacher and hard-nosed psychologist, she promises to transform those flagging sales into big profit-making lines. And she is not cheap. Just one talk can leave an American company little change from $10,000, while for those working in Britain, fees of between £500,000 and £1 million to run a programme seem to be the norm.

A quick check via that modern instant internet communicator – Google – reveals that one American retail motivator, Debbie Allen, is a Gold Stars speaker prepared, for up to $9,999, to reveal from her book, *Trade Secrets of Retail Stars*, or her other book, *Confessions of Shameless Self-Promoters: all you need to know to get 'skyrocketing sales'*. As her puff says: 'These shared success secrets will get you on the fast track to big profits in your business.'

Of course, in dear old Blighty we don't use such a crude

approach as Debbie's – honoured as one of the 'Top 50 Women Business owners of Arizona'. Britain has its own retail motivator, Mary Gober – a New Yorker acclaimed modestly as 'the most dynamic force in customer service culture development today'. She has been established in the US for twenty-six years but now has an office in the UK. And her client list is expanding. Reuters, Novotel Europe, HSS, a hire service company in England and Ireland, and two housing associations, Northern Counties and London Quadrant, are all on her books. There was also a *Daily Mail* article about her in November.

But her biggest company this year has undoubtedly been dear old M&S – once known for sensible underwear and suits – which recently completely lost its way. For a £1 million personal fee and up to another £9 million for other costs, all M&S's staff have been summoned to Birmingham's National Exhibition Centre for a day's 'work training'. Feasted on a breakfast of unlimited M&S coffee, croissants and orange juice, 5,000 staff at a time were encouraged by dynamic Mary to 'dress down' and dance in the aisles as part of a 'feel good' training session.

Some stores really entered into the spirit and came dressed in anything from the Newcastle football strip to jeans and yellow fluorescent jackets like road labourers from Trafford. Each went away with a real one-dollar bill (don't pass the buck when you are serving customers), a gold starfish, and a credit card-sized plastic card which they had to sign. It says: 'I demonstrate our Service Style by consistently being positive, taking ownership and responsibility, being respectful and being determined.'

So next time you are in an M&S store, approach your sales assistant and check them out. If they are rude or don't give you immediate attention, ask to see their signed pledge on that bit of white plastic. If they don't rush to check the stockroom for that skirt size that's not on the hanger, remind them of Mary Gober's little booklet which tells them how they should act.

In other words, see if these expensive retail motivators are real value for money.

*David Hencke*

# Rhubarb Triangle

Many readers will be aware of the Bermuda Triangle, that area of sea between Bermuda, Florida and Puerto Rico which is said to be a region of profound danger to anyone entering it. Readers are also likely to have heard of the Sunni Triangle, another dangerous region reputedly controlled by 'insurgents' in Iraq. But the Rhubarb Triangle, well, that's a different kettle of fish entirely. It is an area where visitors are assured of a friendly welcome, particularly during Wakefield's annual Festival of Rhubarb, which takes place every spring.

The Triangle is an area bordered by Wakefield, Leeds and Bradford where rhubarb has been commercially grown for over 125 years. In its heyday there were over 200 growers producing sufficient rhubarb to justify the running of a daily special train known as the Rhubarb Express. This daily consignment to the wholesale fruit and vegetable markets of London continued until 1962, when transportation by train was substituted by road.

In this tightly knit area, a large percentage of the early crop is cultivated in specially constructed low buildings known as forcing sheds. These windowless, pitch-dark, heated premises, approximately 200 ft long and 10 ft high to the ridge, create ideal conditions for the rhubarb to develop. Depending upon the amount of heat used, it can grow audibly, to those attuned to hear it, at the rate of an inch a day. Being raised in darkness is an important element in the forcing cycle as it preserves the cerise colour of the rhubarb sticks.

During the Second World War, it became part of the staple diet on account of its ready availability – many children being literally force-fed rhubarb. This resulted in a generation that grew up hating the stuff, and from the 1950s onwards there was a rapid decline in its consumption. Many growers went bankrupt, and from that time onwards it fell into such disdain that the word was frequently used as a response to people who spoke inconsequentially – 'Rhubarb, rhubarb!' The word appeared very often in Hansard during that period, although its inclusion was not particularly helpful to rhubarb growers.

Things were going from bad to worse when, eight years ago, the Wakefield Metropolitan Council Tourism Committee came up with a themed annual event which they named the Wakefield Festival of Rhubarb. Launched with eye-catching slogans such as 'Wakefield Talks Rhubarb' and 'Join the Rhubarb Trail', visitors were invited into the mysterious world of the Yorkshire Rhubarb Triangle.

This unusual promotion has been an unqualified success. It has resulted in a reversal of the downward trend, much to the surprise and pleasure of the growers, who are now struggling to meet the demand. Largely as a result of the council-led initiative, rhubarb is enjoying a culinary renaissance. Its low calories and high calcium content appeal to the growing band of individuals with an interest in healthy eating. It has featured in myriad celebrity chef programmes, and some superchefs have elevated rhubarb to much the same position in the culinary league as that once humble but now much vaunted comestible, the fishcake.

This trend has been eagerly latched on to by enterprising restaurateurs, and doubtless an element of inverted snobbery on the part of pompous restaurant reviewers has contributed to the upsurge in demand. But at least the Rhubarb Triangle, unlike other well-known triangles, can be entered without fear for one's personal safety.

*Alan Thomas*

**Modern tongue**

## Dumbing downers

- **Back-to-back**
  (Is 'consecutively' too high-falutin'?)
- **The run-up to Christmas**
  (Previously known as 'Advent'.)
- **Pre-booking**
  (What other kind of booking is there?)
- **Young girls**
  (Tautological. Except when used to distinguish from simply 'girls', used these days to mean any woman under the age of forty, because saying woman would just sound too old and uncool . . .)

# Risk Assessment

The Health and Safety industry has spawned a multitude of ludicrous stories that have in turn entertained us or caused us to wring our hands in despair. But nothing is quite as batty as the pseudo-science of the Risk Assessment, and nothing quite as depressing as the amount of time and effort expended in compiling the reams of paperwork such documents demand.

This is how most Risk Assessments (RAs) work: the organiser of the activity in question has to evaluate each component of the task in hand and allocate two scores, usually on a scale of one to four. The first score is their assessment (i.e. guess) of the probability of an accident taking place – one means it is improbable, four means it is near certain to occur, and so on. The second figure measures the severity of the outcome on the same scale, from a minor scrape to major injury or death. RA forms have a grid for each sub-activity, and a final column in which the two scores are multiplied together. Thus a score of 16 (i.e. $4 \times 4$) indicates a near certainty of disaster, presumably reserved for suicide missions. The logic for this arbitrary arithmetic remains a mystery; there could equally be columns for the phase of the moon or the direction of the wind, and the maths could just as well involve addition, elevation to the nth power or integral calculus. Finally, another column is provided for the assessor to write in the appropriate precautionary measure.

Risk Assessments have penetrated the deepest corners of everyday life. Teachers, for example, cannot carry out any activity with their classes more dangerous than sitting still and facing the front without one. Ordinary trips away from school (never mind adventure activities) require individually compiled RAs. Realising that this might be a disincentive for teachers to organise trips, some public attractions are helpfully publishing pro-forma RAs to ease the process. Each sub-activity on offer has to have its own analysis of the risks. These are a few examples picked at random from one local authority's website.

One museum entertains its younger visitors with 'traditional stories and nursery rhymes'; the hazards, rather oddly, are identified as 'poking with mask sticks or tripping on long skirts'. Risk and severity are each assessed at two, with a suggested precaution of 'Verbal warning, one-to-one close supervision'.

In the garden of another attraction, 'bee stings' are identified as a hazard – happily only a 2 × 1 score – and 'verbal instructions about bees and their habits' were recommended. A country park assesses the danger of 'slipping and falling' as a 2 × 1 and helpfully suggests 'verbal warning: no running'. By contrast, the city museum is a positive minefield; whilst the loos rank a measly 1 × 1, the revolving doors offer the young visitor an exciting frisson of danger at 2 × 3, bettered only by the sculpture workshop that delivers a potentially deadly 2 × 4.

To what appalling dangers we unthinkingly subjected our children in the years before Health 'n' Safety was invented!

Below is a not-untypical risk assessment. I'm serious – I have been obliged in the past to prepare RAs barely less ludicrous than this for projects I have been involved in . . .

**Two tales of Risk Assessments:**

A major utility company, facing an investigation by the Environment Agency, had queried where a tape-recorded interview with its employee should take place. These are verbatim extracts from the EA's replies:

'I am unable to arrange for the interview to be conducted at your own offices. It would be remiss of me to put my officer's health and safety at risk. We have identified that the conduct of interviews is a high-risk activity for our officers. Of course, we could bring extra tapes, spare machine etc. to your offices. However, in order to protect my officer's health and safety, it is not practical or safe to carry this amount of equipment with them.'

When the BBC needed a temporary receiving aerial on a tower block in the City for a one-day seminar, it seemed a simple matter to send a man up in the lift to attach the small magnetic base – essentially a car aerial and worth about £15 – to one of the many metal air-conditioners or steel components in the plant area on the roof.

And so it proved, except that the building managers demanded an application form, a health & safety policy, a high-height working certificate, a method statement and a Risk Assessment. The Beeb had to hire an outside contractor at a cost of £250 to carry out the five-minute task – and to compile the fourteen pages of detailed documentation required to obtain the necessary permission.

*Roddy Gye*

*'I can't relax in the country – there aren't any shops!'*

# The Rules

'While a gentleman is speaking to you . . . do not let your eager attention and visible preference betray the flutter of your heart.'

From *A Father's Legacy to his Daughters,* by John Gregory, a popular conduct book of 1774

'On the first date, avoid staring romantically into his eyes. Otherwise he will know that you're planning the honeymoon.'

From *The Rules,* 1995

When it comes to nailing Mr Right, it would seem that little has changed in the last two centuries. Despite universal suffrage, the feminist movement and the vast advances in social and sexual equality, it appears that most women still fantasise about travelling up the aisle with the man of their dreams. And they still look to conduct books to show them the way.

*The Rules: Time-tested Secrets for Capturing the Heart of Mr Right* first appeared in 1995 and quickly became a publishing phenomenon around the world. Its authors, Ellen Fein and Sherrie Schneider, promise that if you follow The Rules, the man you want will not only marry you, 'but feel crazy about you, forever!' Do The Rules, they say, and 'you'll live happily ever after!'

There are thirty-five principal Rules, which range from the coquettish 'Don't Talk to a Man First' and 'Don't Call Him and Rarely Return His Calls' to the somewhat defensive 'Do The Rules, Even When Your Friends and

Parents Think It's Nuts' and the wholly American 'Don't Discuss The Rules with Your Therapist'.

In essence, The Rules state that a woman should always let the man take the lead, as this is the 'natural order of things'. She should never make the first move, never initiate a meeting and never be the first to call. She shouldn't talk too much, or make sarcastic jokes. She should always strive to look her best, even at home on the weekend, and should wear feminine clothes that appeal to men: short skirts, black sheer stockings and low-cut tops. And she should always let him pick up the restaurant bill.

Should your faith in this system ever waver, the book cites numerous examples of women who zealously followed The Rules and now live happily ever after with Mr Dreamboat and their 2.4 children.

Some aspects of The Rules are positive. They encourage women to believe in themselves, to develop their own interests and not sit at home waiting for the phone to ring. But what's alarming is that even the brightest women seem willing to buy into the idea that there's a magic formula to romantic happiness. Intelligent, ambitious friends talk about how long they should wait before calling a man back, or whether he'll feel emasculated if they insist on going Dutch in a restaurant.

It's strange that the Victorian modes of courtship our mothers and grandmothers fought so hard to escape should hold such appeal for a new generation. But perhaps The Rules tap into the deeply ingrained fairytales of knights and ladies, Elizabeth and Darcy, Jane Eyre and Mr Rochester that even educated, modern women find hard to shake off.

Mind you, what the book doesn't tell you is that Rules author Ellen Fein recently filed for divorce from her husband after a sixteen-year marriage . . .

*Emma Harding*

*'I'm sorry, but according to my database you're just one sugar.'*

## Schmoozing

Oldies may be under the impression that people go to drinks parties to have fun, cadge a few sausage rolls and maybe sluice back a snifter or two with friends. Hard-nosed young thrusters of the twenty-first century know otherwise. Parties are for 'schmoozing'.

To schmooze, an intransitive verb, conjugates thus: I do you a favour, you return the compliment, he or she (my rival) is outmanoeuvred. It was originally a Yiddish word, describing a chat at a social gathering, but such innocence has long passed. Its modern meaning is more complex, verging on the sinister. Schmoozing is the grubby, self-serving, back-scratching, shoulder-stabbing, ego-stroking, eyelid-fluttering, career-enhancing business of cosying up to people you believe might be in a position to assist your ascent of the slippery slope. To watch people schmooze is not a pretty sight.

There is an awful lot of it about these days. Maestro schmoozers include Peter Mandelson, Keith Vaz, all modern lawyers, most television executives and a good proportion of the public relations smoothies greasing their way around central London. The entire edifice of New Labour is built on schmoozing. Institutional schmoozing is to be found at the BBC, executives at the bigger charities have been known to indulge, and there have been signs that the Prince of Wales's littler helpers at St James's Palace have also been 'at it' of late.

Schmoozing is a step up from its eighties predecessor,

'networking'. Whereas networking took place in offices and after-work bars, schmoozing is conducted in carpeted drawing rooms and at the sort of international conference dinners attended by Lord Owen, Henry Kissinger and other superannuated politicians and diplomatists. The raw materials of the schmoozing industry are a packed Rolodex or Psion organiser and the sort of breezy familiarity which in better times might have been considered impertinent but is now thought to show initiative and flair.

Schmoozers are shameless about using private events and venues – weddings, funerals and St James's clubs – for professional advancement. They will even go on holiday or spend weekends with people they little like, simply because they could be professionally useful. Schmoozers have no time for 'wasteful' friendships which do not yield fresh business opportunities.

They think nothing of interrupting other people's conversations. If there is someone they want to schmooze with at a book launch or political reception they will jump straight in, seizing their 'target' by the elbow and saying 'Can I have a quiet word?' What will follow is some murmured suggestion, perhaps a proposed introduction to a potential client or the exposition of a troublesome trifle which the 'target' might be able to solve – in exchange for a favour. One of the essentials of the game is that schmoozers must 'bring something to the table'. That is, they must be able to trade high-level assistance, be it the telephone number of a well-placed Whitehall official or the name of a City headhunter who is looking for 'someone just like you'. It is not so much a case of one good turn *deserving* as *expecting* another. Co-operation and good neighbourliness are regarded not as duties or as an amicable gesture. They are part of the deal.

Schmoozers tend not to drink very much, lest it interfere with their chances of making a 'connection'. Mr Mandelson, for instance, prefers to refresh himself with a *canarino*, a beaker of hot water flavoured by nothing more than a twist of lemon. Lord Levy, Tony Blair's special envoy in the Middle East, is a schmoozer of the first water – but seldom anything stronger.

Schmoozers dress expensively, on the sharp side of traditional, often in Jermyn Street shirts with colour-coded silk ties miraculously free of gravy stains. The male of the species *Schmoozer vulgaris* is uncommonly neat and hygienic in appearance. He remains close-shaven even at the end of a long day and smells faintly of toothpaste and/or Continental cologne. Schmoozers do not sweat, or even glow. Female schmoozers, of whom there are fewer, are less pretty than their male counterparts but equally ruthless. Schmoozers are not long on self-mockery.

There was once a supposition in Britain that the top jobs were awarded on merit. The selection of judges, quangocrats, Government Inquiry chairmen, hospital trustees, Royal Commission members and their ilk were taken on honour as the best men or women for the job. Schmoozing imperils that trust. The cold truth is that these days few public posts are filled without a word or two being muttered out of the side of an influential mouth, without the soft stroking of reputations, the mutual burnishing of prospects and the squeeze of an elbow at a high-octane party coinciding with that enticing phrase, 'Can I have a quiet word . . . ?'

*Quentin Letts*

*'. . . and the lifetime achievement award for the most ASBO nominations goes to . . .'*

# Slow Food

In today's kitchen, time is of the essence. The average person spends twenty minutes preparing their evening meal, assembling ingredients that have travelled an average of 2,000 miles. Huge numbers of us would rather subject our palates to the over-salted, cellophane-wrapped ready meal than face the weary peel, peel, chop, chop required to construct a similar dish ourselves. The British are particularly culpable: we spend as much money on ready meals as all the other EU countries combined.

Food, and fast food in particular, has never been so prominent in national politics. The worldwide obesity epidemic has become a media obsession. Our television schedules are weighed down with rotund celebrities sweating on step machines, while the Government expresses concern that 8.5 per cent of six-year-olds are obese. And in the wake of CJD, GM crops and foot-and-mouth, consumers demand information on the origin and preparation of their food.

The combination of these concerns has led to a mounting backlash against our fast-food culture. In Italy this became an organised movement in 1986, when the Slow Food Association was formed in response to the opening of a McDonald's restaurant near the Spanish Steps in Rome. It now has over 60,000 members based in 46 countries, who are united under the movement's symbol – a snail.

The Association's manifesto declares that it is

committed to the 'protection of the right to taste'. Slow Food's founder, Carlo Petrini, argues in his recent book, *Slow Food: The Case for Taste*, that if consumers are educated in taste, the food industry will be forced to change to accommodate their new demands. If consumers were to start questioning the ingredients, Petrini explains, production and preparation of the food they were buying, food producers themselves might take these questions more seriously. So the movement is committed to traditional ways of growing, producing and preparing food, eschewing the homogenisation of flavour and erosion of local cultures brought about by the developed world's hunger for immediacy.

Slow Food's Italian roots are very apparent in its focus on the pleasures of eating – its place in family and social life, its cultural heritage and its relationship with the landscape. At a local level, the movement takes the shape of 'Convivia' – forums for members to gather and partake of slow food and wine. It's not all self-indulgence, however, as members also discuss food-related issues and support local producers. In Britain the movement has been, er, slow to catch on. Which seems strange for a country that gave the world the Lancashire hotpot, shepherd's pie and Aunt Agatha's slow-boiled Brussels sprouts.

The Slow Food movement has its own publishing company, Slow Food Editore. It has just opened the first 'slow food' university – the University of Gastronomic Science in Pollenza, Piedmont. Another of the movement's projects is the 'Ark of Taste' – a catalogue of foods, dishes and animals that are in danger of disappearing. The list includes Dorset Blue Vinney cheese, Newlyn pilchards and Irish smoked salmon.

Slow Food's battle cry has been taken up in other fields: there is now 'slow fashion', which aims to reinstate the relationship between wearer and garment-maker, and 'slow business', which promotes more effective time management and less presenteeism – where workers stay late at the office in order to earn brownie points.

Even McDonald's recent advertising campaigns have begun to stress their healthier, fresher products, such as salads. Perhaps the Order of the Snail is, slowly, making itself heard.

*Emma Harding*

# Spam

Need some cut-price Viagra? I'm your man. Penis extension surgery? I can put you in touch with an expert. Height enhancement? I know a chap with a rack. Mortgages and loans for those with bad credit ratings? Just an email away, old fruit. I should stress that I'm not the sort of person who consorts regularly with doctors who make liberal use of their prescription pads, or genitally fixated plastic surgeons, or loan sharks. They seek me out, emailing me with offers of the goods and services outlined.

This is 'spam' – the online equivalent of junk mail.

The term is believed to have originated in the early days of the Internet, when a Monty Python obsessive bombarded several online discussion groups with lengthy messages consisting entirely of a repetitive quote from the 'Spam' sketch. Thus, sending useless messages became known as 'spamming'. (Hormel Foods, the manufacturers of the canned luncheon meat of the same name, seem to have taken the hijacking of their trademark philosophically.)

Given that the main purpose of the Internet seems to be the dissemination of pornography, it will come as no surprise that some of the most vigorous spammers are selling sex, as well as the accessories and modifications mentioned above.

Sometimes, a piece of spam can actually provoke a laugh, although this is usually unintentional. Recently, I was offered the chance to 'WORK FROM HOME!' (which

I do anyway) by someone called Pele. Not *the* Pele? Can an international footballer work from home? Imagine the scene at the 1970 World Cup: 'Where's Pele? At home practising dribbles in the garden. He never was a team player.' Shortly after that, I was offered a 'Keep God in the Pledge' T-shirt. It took me a web search to discover that the slogan referred to the campaign to keep God's name in the US Pledge of Allegiance, rather than a link-up between the Church and furniture polish manufacturers.

What kind of idiot would respond to these kinds of emails? Well a recent security flaw in the website of Amazing Internet, a company that sold penis enlargement pills, unwittingly revealed the answer: over a four-week period, some 6,000 people responded to the spam message (subject line: 'Make your penis HUGE'), and bought on average two bottles of herbal penis enlargement pills, at $50 each. The customers included the manager of a $6 million mutual fund, several company directors, a chiropractor, a veterinarian, and a number of military personnel.

It's good to know that in this hi-tech world, there's still one born every minute . . .

*Louis Barfe*

# Speed Dating

'Want to meet new people?' the speeddater.co.uk website asks. 'Too busy to date?' Never fear – the latest kind of drive-thru, instant romantic gratification is at hand.

There are currently 11 million single adults in the UK and this figure is predicted to increase to 16 million by 2010. It's claimed that one in five of these singletons uses a dating service – another figure that seems set to rise.

The commodification of romance has given rise to a bewildering range of dating options. But each has its flaws. Submitting a personal ad requires witty and concise self-summation, as well as the ability to translate vast strings of arcane abbreviations. And what happens when you can no longer truthfully declare 'OHOT' (own hair, own teeth)? Using a dating agency generally requires sitting out a succession of painful dates with unsuitable partners, and though the Internet has the advantage of anonymity this can also make it the refuge of the truly weird. But if you're determined to bite the bullet, you might consider the latest addition to the fold – speed dating.

This is how it works: large numbers of men and women descend on a stylish, upmarket venue. The women sit at individual tables and each is joined by a man, her first 'date'. After three minutes of conversation, a bell rings and the man moves on to the next table. Both parties mark on a scorecard whether they wish to see that person again – the twenty-first-century equivalent of marking one's dance card. At the end of the evening, the organisers collate the results, inform participants of any matches and provide contact email addresses.

The concept of speed-dating naturally originates across the Atlantic. A Manhattan rabbi came up with the idea in order to help New Yorkers find compatible Jewish partners. Its popularity was fuelled on both sides of the Atlantic when it was featured in the American TV show *Sex and the City*.

Many might be intimidated by the pressure to dazzle in just three minutes. But speed dating is based on the principle that most of us make a judgment about someone within the first few seconds of a meeting. Presumably this rests on the biological premise that every encounter with another creature raises three basic questions: Can I eat it? Can it eat me? Do I want to have sex with it? (Or, in the case of some species of spider, all three.)

For humans, though, the allotted time of a speed date requires some verbal dexterity. A number of speed daters have reported that many of the three-minute conversations revolve around the size of the venue and the strangeness of only having three minutes to get to know each other. Fascinating stuff. Who said romance was dead?

*Emma Harding*

## Spiritual Intelligence

First there was IQ, the intelligence quotient, a figure which indicates your potential to stand up to the interrogations of Anne Robinson. Then there was EQ, emotional intelligence, a concept made popular by Daniel Goleman's 1995 bestselling book of the same name, which emphasised the importance of the emotions in decision-making and personal success.

And thus, inevitably, was born SQ, or 'spiritual intelligence'. This refers to the skills and behaviours necessary to be at one with the world. When you are spiritually intelligent you are more aware of your place and purpose within the universe and consequently exhibit greater consideration for your fellow man. Some claim that SQ is the most important of our various intelligences, with the power to transform not only one's own life, but the very course of history. Nothing like thinking big.

So how should you set about developing your spiritual intelligence? The first step is to venture into the self-help section of your local bookshop – that's the one where the dust jackets are entirely filled by the books' lengthy, optimistic titles: *7 Habits of Highly Effective People*; or *Excuse Me, Your Life is Waiting: The Astonishing Power of Feelings*, for example. The lettering on these covers is usually gold and in a large, clear font, suggesting that people who buy the books must be a) in need of some gilt and sparkle in their lives, and b) not the brightest spoon in the jamjar.

One such book, dedicated to the study of SQ, is entitled

*The Power of Spiritual Intelligence: 10 Ways to Tap Into Your Spiritual Genius*, by Tony Buzan, billed on his dust jacket (purple with gold lettering) as the 'multimillion-copy bestselling author'. To help you get a sense of how spiritually intelligent you are, Buzan provides twenty-nine questions, of which the following are a sample. You may only answer Yes or No – spiritual intelligence clearly does not appreciate equivocators:

Do you feel 'at one' with nature? YES/NO
Do you believe the human race has a true purpose? YES/NO
Do you like animals? Do they respond truly to you? YES/NO
Do you go out of your way to kill flies, bugs, and 'creepy-crawlies'? YES/NO

So if you've just settled down with this book after a morning of spreading ant powder around your doorstep and squirting your roses against greenfly, you can be assured that your path to spiritual intelligence is going to be a long and difficult one.

Why is it that all those who claim to be able to help you on the path to clarity of thought dress up essentially simple ideas in obfuscation? The books and websites which explain spiritual intelligence are awash with bewildering concepts such as 'self-actualisation', 'transpersonal development', 'in the symptom is the soul', 'check your self-talk'. That said, most of the books on spiritual intelligence basically seem to be advocating that we should try to be generous, honest, compassionate, considerate of others and of the world we live in. They suggest spiritual exercises such as providing a sympathetic ear to a friend in need, or sticking by a promise to keep a personal secret confidential. Isn't this just called 'being nice'?

*Emma Harding*

**Modern tongue**

### Like, massively annoying, No 1

- Work–life balance
- You're invading my personal space
- Comfort zone
- Wake-up call
- 24/7

# Sudoku

Sudoku. The very sound is exotic – a lot more exotic than one would expect from a small grid of numbers. Or rather, a small grid with just a few numbers and a lot of infuriating blank spaces. For Sudoku is not a cunning new development in Feng Shui or an amazing hands-on complementary therapy involving salty mud and betel nuts. No, it is a puzzle. A logic puzzle. And it is everywhere.

There are eighty-one squares, laid out as nine blocks of nine, and the aim of the game is to complete the grid so that each block contains the numbers one to nine. And each row of the grid contains the numbers one to nine. And each column of the grid contains the numbers one to nine. And that's it. You don't even have to be able to count from one to nine, you just need to be able to think logically.

Now before we simply accept that puzzles are the new rock and roll and move on, perhaps it would be best to examine just how bizarre a notion this is. This is a puzzle that requires nothing in the way of language skills, numeracy or general knowledge. Only the rigorous application of logic will ensure that the 'puzzlee' does not mess the whole thing up and have to copy it all out on a piece of squared paper and start again.

Who knew that the British public was crying out for a concrete means of expression for its logical reasoning powers? You'd never have guessed from *Pop Idol*'s viewing figures. Premium-rate phone lines are available to offer hints on solving today's challenge; books are being sold and, as with all of modern life, you can play it on your mobile phone.

Until last year you will, like as not, never have seen a Sudoku puzzle and now you cannot escape them. Where have they come from?

Despite the exotically oriental name, it seems that the roots of Sudoku lie in the famously lively hills of Switzerland. One can even imagine Julie Andrews cunningly weaving its pronunciation into song: sue-doe-coo – 'Sue, a boy, a boy called Sue etc.' Oh no, wait, that was Austria. Pity.

In those days, Sudoku was apparently called Magic Squares and was simpler and smaller and a lot less de rigueur. From there, it was picked up by a Japanese publishing company, given a quick makeover and a new name. The puzzle's success in Japan was duly noted by one of those global whizzkids whose job it is to notice this sort of thing, and Sudoku was brought to our shores. It seems that the *Daily Mail* and the *Times* still squabble over which of them saw it first.

Sudoku now comes in many forms, from 'easy' to 'fiendish', depending upon the number and location of squares that are completed for you. A casual passing interest, dabbling with a few 'easy' days, has the effect of an alcopop on a vulnerable teenager, quickly leading on to harder stuff. The subsequent despair that envelops the soul when one launches unsuspectingly into one's first 'fiendish' puzzle is not a pretty thing.

Early side-effects of Sudoku are already surfacing. My mother claims she can polish off a 'fiendish' in the blink of an eye, but I have noticed that when puzzling away, she develops the 'Sudoku stare', with its characteristic marked reduction in eye movement. In fact, her blink rate is reduced to once every four hours. Perhaps Optrex should consider a sponsorship deal?

*Eleanor Hill*

*'Feng Shui on Mondays, yoga on Wednesdays, Tai Chi on Tuesdays and Thursdays – what a stressful life you lead.'*

# Supersizing

If you've eaten in a fast-food restaurant in the past decade the chances are that you've been supersized. Or that you've 'Gone Large', or been 'Extra Valued' or 'Meal Dealed' – or basically paid a few pence extra to upgrade your normal-sized meal of 'regular' burger, 'medium' fries and 'small' soft drink to a meal containing a burger the size of your head, a whopping great armful of fries and a drink so large it comes with its own lifeguard.

Supersizing is in many ways the Holy Grail of fast food. The actual foodstuff is the cheapest part of the fast-food equation, so practically every penny of the supersize premium is profit. It is also irresistible to us consumers – for an extra 30p or so on a £3 meal, you would be almost doubling the size of your burger, chips and drink. Yum.

There is just one drawback to this win-win situation of chips-on-the-cheap: along with our meals, our waistlines have also been getting supersized. Burgers, fries and fizzy drinks have never exactly been the cornerstone of a balanced diet, but at least when fast-food giant McDonald's first opened in the 1950s, its burger, fries and 12-oz Coca-Cola totalled 590 calories. The American organisation the National Alliance for Nutrition and Activity found that, in comparison, a Supersized Extra Value McDonald's meal in 2003 – quarter-pounder with cheese, supersize fries and supersize Coke – weighed in at a massive 1,550 calories and contained over 40 grams of saturated fat.

What is particularly damaging to our waistlines (and our hearts and livers) is that with a supersized portion of just about anything, you almost always get a disproportionate rise in calories and saturated fat for the extra cost. McDonald's small to large fries: 62 per cent more money buys you 157 per cent more calories; small to medium unbuttered popcorn in a cinema: 23 per cent more money buys you 125 per cent more calories. Add to this our well-documented compulsion to eat up everything that's put before us, and it's little wonder that 60 per cent of Americans fall into the category of 'overweight' or 'obese', and that UK health officials are now talking in terms of an 'obesity time bomb'.

However, the writing appears to be already on the wall for supersizing (albeit writing obscured by lots of obese people standing in the way). McDonald's recently announced that it was discontinuing its supersizing offers. Lack of consumer interest was cited as the main reason, although it did admit that a focus on healthier eating was also a concern. It's likely that increasingly bad press may also have had something to do with it: in 2003 two girls in the USA sued McDonald's for 'causing their obesity'. (The case was thrown out, but not before the judge had branded McDonald's chicken nuggets a 'McFrankenstein creation of various elements not utilised by the home cook'.)

Just prior to McDonald's decision to stop supersizing, the film *Supersize Me* was released, in which Morgan Spurlock, a fit and healthy 33-year-old film-maker, documented what happened to him when he lived only on McDonald's food for a month, accepting supersized portions when they were offered to him. He catalogued the resulting devastation of his health – vomiting, depression, near liver failure and a gain of almost two stone were just some of the effects.

So hoorah! Supersizing appears to be a thing of the past. Only the other day I saw an advertisement on the telly from Kentucky Fried Chicken advertising salads as the new cool fast food.

But it isn't all good news. Have you noticed the rise of 'all you can eat' buffet restaurants recently? Where our waistlines are concerned, the real enemy isn't supersizing, it's our own insatiable desire for a bargain, combined with that well-known urge to clear our plates. If McDonald's won't supersize us, we'll supersize ourselves.

*Nick Parker*

# Tamagotchi

It is the holy grail of marketing. Find a product that no one needs, that no one wants, but that everyone will be willing to pay absurd sums of money for, even though it doesn't do anything and costs almost nothing to make. Marketing men sit every day at small hardboard desks in glass hutches on the fourth floors of huge gleaming headquarters in Maidenhead, dreaming of just such a product. But the Hula Hoop is long gone, the Spice Girls are ancient history. What is needed is something technological, something electronic . . . something tamagotchi.

A tamagotchi is a miraculous bit of nonsense. An unsophisticated little computer chip packed into a multicoloured plastic case to make it look as cheap as possible, but actually costing about thirty-five quid. In effect, it's a sort of computer game. When you switch it on, the Tamagotchi doesn't do very much, but you as its owner must ensure that it 'eats' and 'sleeps' and so 'stays alive'. All this requires attention, which itself requires time, which is the most precious of modern commodities. So if you briefly forget about your tamagotchi, it ceases to thrive, and after severe and constant neglect it eventually 'dies'. Good news you would have thought, you can now chuck it in the bin. Not a bit of it. These repulsive little items seem to get under everybody's skin.

We may all evade as much responsibility as possible in real life, but owners of tamagotchis all become frantic to keep their charges in the rudest of electronic health. You can never succeed with a tamagotchi, for there is no final achievement. You can only ever fail. This is a computer game which you can never win, but can all too easily lose. It's an ingenious form of torture. Only the Japanese would ever have thought of it.

And if adults are so pathetically susceptible, what of children, the tamagotchi's real target market? The Pied Piper of Hamelin was no fool: his modern-day equivalent would probably be working for Nintendo. Many kids have become obsessed. Passers-by, studying tinies in the depths of tamagotchi trance, probably assumed that they were out of their heads on ecstasy or glue. If they had been, they would probably have been more sociable. Parents could not believe that their children were capable of such rapt concentration. Their schoolwork may have suffered, but at least the little darlings were quiet. One couple I know said they hadn't slept so well in years.

And then as quickly as the craze started, it finished. What did for tamagotchi was oversupply. Encouraged by sales and media response, Japan flooded the market. Soon you could buy tamagotchis for £6.99 in Tescos. So now nobody wants to know. Eight-year-olds turn their barely visible noses up at them. They may just about admit to having a tamagotchi six months ago but they certainly don't have one now. Don't even suggest it. It's just not something we talk about.

The holy grail of marketing? It was for a fortnight. In Japan the marketing men scratch their heads and plan the tamagotchi revival . . .

*Marcus Berkmann*

# TOG

For once, Chamber's, Webster's and the Oxford dictionaries are of one mind: 'TOGs: Terry's Old Geezers/Gals, listeners to "Wake Up To Wogan", 7.30–9.30 am, Monday to Friday, BBC Radio 2. Thought to be in direct line of descent from the TWITS (Terry Wogan Is Tops Society), a movement which enjoyed "a far, fierce hour and sweet" and burned out, just as quickly! Rather like Wogan himself . . .'

Like the aforementioned, once-proud broadcaster, TOGs are well-stricken in years, while remaining about twenty-five years old on the inside. They have a fierce resentment of anybody younger than themselves ('They don't know they're born!') and are loath to allow them into their purlieus: 'Clear off, you young limb!' is the rallying cry.

TOGs usually come in flat caps, Volvos and the centre lane of the motorway at 60 mph ('I'm within my rights; 50 mph on the inside, 70 on the outside and 60 in the middle . . .'). They have a secret sign, known only to those who hear it flashed, rather like some Bat-Signal, on the radio every morning.

There is an even more secret Grand Master, or Togmeister, sign – always exchanged under cover of darkness or the snug of a seedy pub near Broadcasting House – which is known only to Wogan himself, the ailing producer Pauly Walters and the Duke of Kent. TOGs may also be recognised by their use of such arcane phrases as 'Is it me?', or 'I never saw a bar of chocolate until I was 14', or 'What am I doing, standing here in front of an open fridge, with a torch in my hand?'

Many thousands of TOGs car stickers have been sent to eager applicants, who, once they receive them, get cold feet and hide them in the back of an upstairs drawer. Those brave enough to flaunt the sticker in the back window of their Reliant Robin or Morris Mini Traveller pay a terrible price, not only in loss of face among nearest, dearest and the rest of the population, but in the trade-in value: the thing is impossible to remove.

The TOGs sweater, which, like the car sticker, is rarer than hen's teeth, bears the legend, 'Do I come here often?' – a tried and trusted TOG chat-up line. There was a strong groundswell of opinion to have 'I stop for no particular reason' on the back, but it soon petered out. Currently a movement is gathering strength to have the logos changed to 'It's never your fault' on the front and 'Mustn't grumble' on the back. It will come to nothing. They'll forget about it if you don't pay any attention. This condition is know to TOGs as a 'senior moment', a euphemism culled from the USA, to indicate a temporary loss of all marbles by anyone over fifty.

As is the current practice within the BBC itself, TOGs feel a deep-seated need to form themselves into groups, clusters or tribes. Witness this letter from a well-set-up woman from Norfolk:

'We decided to start our own local branch of TOGs and the very first meeting took place last week. The session started with a game, to break the ice, of I-Spy. This proved to be a mistake because most of the members had forgotten to bring their glasses. Undeterred, we decided to be more daring – the men then threw their false teeth into the middle of the carpet and the ladies had to pick a denture and pair off with its owner. They then adjourned to other rooms to discuss their operations. We ended with a raffle, first prize of which was a knitted pension-book cover . . .'

But I see that you are all eagerness: 'How do I become a TOG?' Be of good cheer. You're in. Welcome to the club.

*Terry Wogan*

*'Remind me – am I getting up or going to bed?'*

# Transparency

See what we are doing! There's nothing in our hands! Nothing up our sleeves! Trying to pull the wool over your eyes? No we are not! How can we be doing anything underhand? We are transparent! Yes we are! Which is why we work in offices that look like greenhouses! You can see right in! No funny business! Not us!

We used to require our politicians to be open and truthful, whereas these days we stipulate 'transparency'. Presumably we are all now so cynical that when presented with a politician, we assume we must be able to 'see through' them . . .

*Nick Parker*

*'The policy of diversity and social inclusion has really gone tits up.'*

# Tribute Band

Imitation is the sincerest form of flattery. In the world of popular music, it is also the surest way of making up for a lack of personal creativity. In a long history of bands doing cover versions of famous songs, there has rarely been any excuse for bothering. Madonna's karaoke-style slaughter of Don Maclean's 'American Pie' is as good an example as any.

Fans of Elvis Presley have been flattering the King in a slightly different way for years. Not content with just doing versions of his songs, many have donned false sideburns and flared jumpsuits and done full-blown impersonations. There have been fat Elvises, thin Elvises, girl Elvises, Punjabi Elvises. There is a restaurant on the Old Kent Road where a Chinese Elvis serenades you as you eat your chow mein.

It was a while, though, before the idea to impersonate a whole band occurred to anybody. In 1980, the ex-cast of the Beatles-inspired musical *Beatlemania* realised that there was a great demand for all things Fab Four, and they formed the Bootleg Beatles, wearing period sixties costumes, playing vintage instruments, and emulating the sound and the look of the Beatles note for painstaking note. It is arguable that they count as the first tribute band, but the Beatles are such a part of national culture, and the Bootlegs' show is such a theatrical attempt to recreate the sixties, that it has as much in common with a Heritage Day at a National Trust property as with a rock concert.

The true birth of the tribute band was in Australia in 1989. Being thousands of miles away from the centre of the pop universe, Australia was rarely visited by big-name acts, and musician Rod Leissle decided that if Oz couldn't have the real thing, then copycat versions would do just as well. To this end he formed Björn Again, a 'tribute' to the seventies Swedish pop sensation Abba. He quickly found fans. Before the end of the year his band were playing five nights a week. Other tribute bands followed: the Australian Doors resurrected the memory of Jim Morrison and his archetypal American rockers; Elton Jack brought Elton John's music to the Antipodes. The phenomenon spread around the world, and very soon there were hundreds of tribute bands, celebrating the music of bands as diverse as Queen (The Royal Family), Pink Floyd (Think Floyd) and Take That (Fake That).

It is easy to see the appeal of tribute bands. They allow you to see bands or artists previously denied to you by virtue of the fact that they are dead. At last, rock 'n' roll-style fatalities through drug overdoses or plane crashes need no longer be a disaster for your fans. Instead of paying £30 to sit at the back of a draughty football stadium in Milton Keynes and watch the Rolling Stones hobble around the stage as specks on the horizon, you can see the youthful Rolling Clones strut the stage at your local pub for a fiver and share a drink with them after. (Admittedly, there's no point in asking for their autographs.) Tribute bands are generally not concerned with artistic merit or creativity, which means you get to listen to all the really great crowd-pleasing 'early period' songs without having to sit through the dull 'experimental' tunes or the guff off the latest album that nobody is really bothered about anyway.

The world of pop music has always thrived on image and inauthenticity, and unsurprisingly tribute bands have fitted right in, and developed an interesting sub-culture of their own: recently, tribute bands of acts who are still very much alive and gigging have started to spring up, and No Way Sis, a tribute to Manc rockers Oasis, who started 'paying tribute' just a few months after the original Oasis became famous, even released their own 'original' Oasis-style songs. When pop band Erasure released some Abba-inspired songs on an EP called Abbaesque, Björn Again released some Erasure-inspired songs called Erasureish. An ex-member of the now defunct Stone Roses has been spotted playing with a Stone Roses tribute band.

There is little doubt that the copycat acts are here to stay. They have become a multi-billion-pound industry. The Bootleg Beatles regularly play in front of tens of thousands of fans at rock festivals, and Björn Again can sell out multiple nights at the Albert Hall. Some tribute bands sell out months in advance. How long, in fact, before the first tribute band spawns a tribute band of its own? After all, the facsimile of the copy of the show must go on . . .

*Nick Parker*

## Tweenagers

There's nothing more flattering than finding out you've become a target market. We all complain that we've become 'just a number', that we're more complex individuals than any marketing strategy can imply and all that, but secretly it makes us feel important. It is a sign that we (or at least our wallets) wield a certain amount of power, that our concerns are more likely to be listened to, even if only for the reason that those who listen the closest are more likely to get their hands on our cash. Recently, it has become the turn of anyone aged between eight and twelve to feel powerful, for they are now officially 'tweenagers'.

In case you are in any doubt as to whether any of your own grandchildren are tweenagers, here are a few pointers.

All tweenagers love mobile phones. Whether they own one or not – and over half of them do – they will be able to recite the coolest make and model numbers in excruciating detail, rather as children in the past could recite train numbers or cricket scores. They will spend a considerable amount of time text-messaging each other across the playground ('whr r u?' 'by tck shp' – the nine-year-old's version of 'Hi, I'm on the train').

Tweenagers have learned many things from television. Look for the following signs: a knowledge of how to slay vampires (*Buffy the Vampire Slayer*); an ability to insult you in black American ghettospeak ('Talk to the hand, 'cos the face don't wanna know ya' – *The Jerry Springer Show*); a frighteningly adult knowledge combined with a naivety that reveals their true age: (on hearing on the news that Monica Lewinsky had given the President of the United States a blow job, a tweenager asks, 'Mummy, what's a President?').

Tweenage boys love Play Stations, X boxes, Pokémon and expensive trainers. Tweenage girls love their friends and shopping, shopping, shopping. The power of tweenage-girl pocket money (plus a little of the parental blackmail which is known in marketing terms as 'pester power') has produced a boom in tweenage ranges. The trinket and bauble shop Claire's Accessories, launched just five years ago, now has stores in practically every town and city in the country. Boots and Superdrug have followed their lead by producing tweenie brands of make-up, bath and beauty products.

The tweenager is the inevitable result of time-honoured childhood passions – having gangs of friends, playing games, dressing up – meeting an advancing technological and consumer culture. There are now far more things for youngsters to buy, and more money than ever to buy it with – couples are having fewer children, often later in life, so there is more disposable income to go round.

But it is technology that has arguably made the biggest difference, with television allowing the young to share more and more in the adult world. It is noteworthy that favourite tweenage shows such as *Friends* and *The*

*Simpsons* are adult favourites as well. Not just mobile phones but also the Internet have allowed tweenagers to communicate with each other and with the adult world to an unprecedented degree.

And there is some evidence that tweenagers are literally growing up faster. A recent study by the Bristol Institute of Child Health showed that one in six girls and one in fourteen boys were showing signs of puberty by the time they were eight years old. The *Times* recently reported that anecdotal evidence from parents and teachers showed a marked increase in the amount of children starting puberty while still at junior school. And although there are likely to be other factors at work (obesity in particular is linked to the early onset of puberty, and obesity rates among children are rising), scientists have by no means ruled out the effect of socialisation on the onset of puberty.

You may think that your nine-year-old granddaughter, dressed like a Spice Girl, talking hip American slang and playing Snake 2 on her Nokia, would have no need for a grandparent who is bewildered by her behaviour. Not so: after all, you are an experienced 'grey pounder' yourself, and as such have the knowledge of how to survive in the consumer minefield of Buy One Get One Free, of You Have Been Specially Chosen, and of Would You Like Our Insurance Cover With That? This information needs passing on to the younger generation as a matter of urgency.

*Nick Parker*

## Visitor Centre

A few years ago, tramping through the undergrowth in Epping Forest, I stumbled across a clearing in which was situated the Epping Forest Visitor Centre. Inside was a short corridor covered with fake bits of tree made from old toilet rolls, with leaves cut of out cardboard and painted by schoolchildren. Visitors were invited to walk up and down in order to experience what it might be like to walk through a real forest. Honestly, there weren't even any badges saying 'I've experienced the Epping Forest Experience'.

Most visitor centres used to be this bad. But not any more. Thanks to lottery funding, an infatuation with technology and our new-found love of quality coffee, many visitor centres have now been transformed from simple wooden huts requesting a 50p donation and offering a meagre array of souvenir pencil sharpeners to fully interactive virtual reality wonderlands. With coffee bars. And hefty admission prices.

The most recent visitor centre to get an upgrade is the one at Whitby Abbey, North Yorkshire. The Whitby Abbey Headland Project has replaced the old ramshackle visitor centre with a state-of-the-art glass box suspended within the ruins of the medieval abbey. The architects of this £5.7 million cube, Stanton Williams, were particularly anxious not to destroy the 'unique melancholy atmosphere' of the site. 'That's why we put grey mesh blinds behind the windows,' they said. But they needn't have worried – thanks to great leaps in the construction of virtual reality, it is rumoured that the centre is soon to be fitted with a revolutionary 'melancholy atmosphere experience': visitors will be able to pay £25 to sit inside a lead box, in which special mood-altering lasers will make one feel exactly the sort of wistful introspection that walking around the grounds of a deserted ruin would have induced before a visitor centre was erected in the middle of it. Until then, however, visitors will just have to make do with the mildly unsettling glumness that can be obtained by shelling out £9 for a family ticket.

Also on the cards for a major overhaul is the visitor centre at Stonehenge. This will be timed to coincide with some long overdue work to sink the obtrusive A303 – which runs just a hundred or so yards from the stones – into an underground tunnel. The visitor centre will also be situated a good mile from the site, leaving the stones in splendid isolation.

The trouble with splendid isolation, however, is that it's not much of a money-spinner, so English Heritage has been looking at ways of increasing revenue. Past ideas have included siting a McDonald's restaurant at the centre, and also constructing a complete replica 'henge indoors. ('It will probably be more attractive to many tourists. The Wiltshire downlands are often wet and cold,' remarked Claire Prout, Druid and site adviser, back in January 2000.) But ultimately, none of these schemes has been deemed exciting enough, and as such we can exclusively reveal that, upon its opening in a few years' time, visitors to the new Stonehenge 'experience' will be privy to the greatest visitor attraction of all time; they will be transported back in time to 3000 BC, to witness the very construction of Stonehenge itself. The price (as yet undecided) will include cappuccinos and a badge saying: 'I've pre-experienced the pre-Stonehenge experience'.

Early time travel trials have revealed that, contrary to what Druids may think about the religious origins of Stonehenge, the site was probably constructed as some kind of visitor centre . . .

*Nick Parker*

**Modern tongue**

## Like, massively annoying, No 2

- Dude
- I was, like, totally . . .
- Whatever
- Cheers, mate
- There you go

# Index

References to entries are indicated in **bold** type